TO
HELL
OR
MONTO

TO
HELL
OR
MONTO

THE STORY OF
DUBLIN'S MOST
NOTORIOUS DISTRICTS

MAURICE CURTIS

The
History
Press
Ireland

First published 2015

The History Press Ireland
50 City Quay
Dublin 2
Ireland
www.thehistorypress.ie

British Library Cataloguing in Publication Data.
A catalogue record for this book is available from the British Library.

ISBN 978 1 84588 863 3

Typesetting and origination by The History Press
Printed and bound in Great Britain by TJ International Ltd. Padstow

CONTENTS

ACKNOWLEDGEMENTS

Many people were helpful in researching this book. Two of the most historic areas of Dublin are covered and consequently I am very grateful to individuals and residents of these areas for their help. Hell was located on the fringes (in more ways than one) of the Liberties, and Councillor John Gallagher of the Liberties Heritage Association was a guiding light and inspiration. He fought the good fight on the Wood Quay issue for decades (see my book *The Liberties*, 2013). He also fought many other battles for the people of his beloved community. In the Monto area, like the Liberties, one individual also stands out – Terry Fagan. A special thanks to Terry and the North Inner City Folklore Project. Terry Fagan is not your typical folklorist; but then again, Dublin's Monto and its people are not typical subjects. Born and reared in Corporation Buildings, the heart of the one-time notorious red-light district, Monto, Terry has written much on the area over the years. 'With all these new developments that are springing up around us, we feel it is important for something to be preserved and documented before the whole place fades into history', he argues. A graduate of the 'Redbrick Slaughterhouse', Rutland Street School, Terry's determination to bring to life the history of this fascinating part of Dublin came to fruition in his writings and history-promoting activities in the area. Terry

Fagan is truly a walking encyclopaedia about all things Monto. Growing up in the area has given him first-hand experience of the many changes, bad and good, visited upon this unique area in Dublin. Not only that but he personifies the distinctive and unquenchable spirit of Monto, a spirit that was much in evidence in 1913, 1916 and the War of Independence, and that has played a hugely important part in modern Irish history. Des O'Hanlon of the famous old historic pub, Cleary's, also made me feel very welcome, as did the Monto Barber on Amiens Street.

Thanks to Alan O'Keefe of the *Herald* for information on Darkey Kelly. Of immeasurable help and inspiration was John Finnegan, who wrote articles on Monto in the *Evening Herald* in April 1972, which subsequently became the book *The Story of Monto*. Likewise my thanks go to Larissa Nolan of the *Irish Independent* and Lisa-Marie Griffith. Eamon McLoughlin, the radio producer of the documentary *No Smoke without Hellfire*, and fellow researcher Phil O'Grady were helpful with information about Darkey Kelly, as was Charles Gregg with his song about Darkey Kelly called 'Second Class Woman'. Karyn Moynihan, of the Women's Museum of Ireland, provided much information on Margaret Leeson. Mary Lyons has done much service, particularly for her work on Margaret Leeson. D. Fallon of the 'Come Here to Me' history blog was helpful on many aspects of Dublin's history. Mark Simpson was helpful for his detailed information on the 'madams' of Monto. Thanks also to Niamh O'Reilly of the Global Women's Studies Programme, NUI Galway, for her documentary *Three Hundred Years of Vice*. I am also grateful to David Ryan and Michael Fewer for their landmark work on the Hellfire Club. Thanks to Maggie Armstrong of the *Irish Independent* for her observations that the squalor and brothels of Monto were a large part of James Joyce's *Ulysses*. Director Louise Lowe and designer Owen Boss of Anu Productions' have done much in recent years with their extraordinary yet disquieting theatrical presentation of a four-part history of Monto called *The Monto Cycle*. Thanks also to Harold Beck and John Simpson for their research on James Joyce; their work on the madams deserves particular praise and I found their notes indispensable. Senator David Norris and Peter Costello added much to my understanding of James Joyce. Grateful thanks in particular to the legendary Oliver St John Gogarty biographer, Ulick O'Connor, for his kind permission to use Gogarty's material. Thanks also to Dr Maire Kennedy in Dublin City Libraries and Archives, and the very helpful staff in Pearse Street Public Library deserve particular gratitude. June O'Reilly, with the able help of Larry and Nuala, was of immense help with her photographic skills. I am very grateful also to Ronan Colgan and Beth Amphlett of The History Press for their constant encouragement, skills and indefatigable patience. Finally, my gratitude goes to the people of the Liberties (wherein Hell is to be found) and Monto for their help, friendliness and encouragement.

INTRODUCTION

This book looks at two of the most infamous and notorious red-light districts in Dublin: Hell and Monto. Hell was the centre of vice, gambling, duelling, rowdy taverns, bawdy houses and other disreputable activities in the eighteenth century. Monto took over the mantle in the late nineteenth and early twentieth centuries. Hell was located along the lanes and alleyways at the front and back of Christ Church Cathedral and extended from Cork Hill, Copper Alley/Fishamble Street, John's Lane East, St Michael's Hill/Skinners Row (now Christ Church Place), Winetavern Street and to Cook Street. Monto was located between Amiens Street and Lower Gardiner Street, between Sean McDermott Street and Lower Talbot Street and only a short walk from O'Connell Street and Dublin Port.

Hell was identified on Rocque's *Map of Dublin, 1756* and the name was in common usage in the eighteenth century and beyond to describe an area of notorious taverns (e.g. Winetavern Street, so called because of the large number of ale and wine houses), brothels and gambling houses that were clustered together, essentially in the shadow of the cathedral and the old walls of Dublin. This was where Dublin's prostitutes, pimps, cutpurses, rakes and murderers houses were to be found. Darkey Kelly, Pimping Peg, Molly Malone, disreputable taverns and coffee-houses as well as the Smock Alley Theatre and the infamous Hellfire Club were all associated with Hell.

Though the name Monto has endured in folk memory, it was not the first major brothel area in Dublin. Hell was equally notorious, feared and renowned in its day. And like Monto, the police (watch) dared not venture in! It was in the early eighteenth century that the cobbled streets and laneways were laid out around Copper Alley, Smock Alley, Fishamble Street and the surrounding area, on land acquired by William Temple (1554–1628). This included the former lands of the Augustinian friary that had stood here for nearly 500 years until the dissolution of the monasteries by Henry VIII. Once the monks had departed the taverners, publicans and prostitutes stepped in, and for a century or so thereafter, until the very late eighteenth century, it and the wider area in the immediate vicinity of Christ Church Cathedral had a very disreputable reputation and were known far and wide as Hell.

Monto took over from Hell with the demolition of the old lanes and alleyways around Christ Church Cathedral in late

Winetavern Street and Christ Church Cathedral in the late 1950s. (Courtesy of GCI)

Chapter Lane in the vicinity of Christ Church Cathedral, 1913. This is typical of the kind of lanes and alleys that were in abundance in Hell. (Courtesy of GCI/harvest)

eighteenth and the early nineteenth centuries. This was the work of the Wide Streets Commissioners, who wished to abolish the old medieval lanes and alleys that dominated old Dublin, and where prostitution flourished. However, their changes just resulted in prostitution moving to new quarters in the city and soon Monto was full of brothels and houses of ill repute. In the late eighteenth and early nineteenth centuries Monto was the most famous red-light district in Dublin, possibly Europe. However, the name 'Monto' never appeared on any map as it was the nickname. The name is derived from Montgomery Street (now called Foley Street), which runs parallel to the lower end of Talbot Street, towards what is now Connolly Station.

The upheaval caused by the 1798 Rebellion, the Act of Union and the abolition of the Irish Parliament in 1800 had a major economic impact on the life of Dublin. The bulk of the city's people forged a precarious existence in high-density, poor-quality housing, surviving on the low incomes earned from casual labour. Ill health was endemic and mortality rates extremely

high. There was large-scale desertion of the city by those associated with the Irish Parliament. Within a decade, many of the
finest mansions (such as Leinster House, Powerscourt House
and Aldborough House) had been sold. Many of the large
four- and five-storey houses in areas such as Gardiner Street,
Buckingham Street, Montgomery and Mecklenburgh Streets
and Summerhill were sold to unscrupulous property developers
and landlords who reduced them to tenements. Many of these
tenements became brothels, and the life and legend that was
Monto was born.

The nineteenth century also saw nearly ten army barracks
located in Dublin. Prostitution derives from poverty and follows
armies as sure as night follows day. Because there was a ready
customer base from the thousands of soldiers stationed in the city,
Monto became, according to a Dublin judge in 1901, 'Europe's
most dreadful den of immorality'.

Strolling in Sackville Street in early 1920s. This area was a favourite meeting place
for Monto prostitutes and soldiers from the many army barracks dotted around
the city. (Courtesy of Dublin Forums/Rashers)

Cover of a religious pamphlett warning about the perils of Hell. (Courtesy of CTSI)

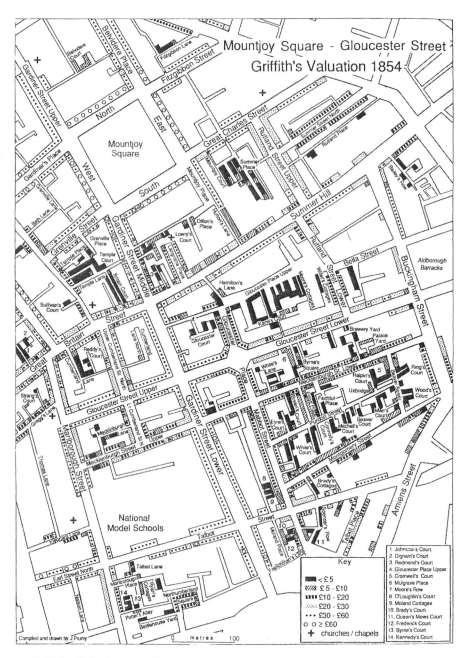

Griffith's Valuation map of Monto and the surrounding area, *c.* 1854. The main district of Monto was in the vicinity of Montgomery and Mecklenburgh Streets. These streets are today called Foley ad Railway Streets respectively. (Courtesy of CSO/GCI)

This book then describes the two most notorious red-light districts not only in Dublin and Ireland but in also in Europe. Both places were renowned throughout the British Empire. Students at Dublin's Trinity College were threatened with penalties if they went near Hell. Another student and in a later time, James Joyce, prowled the streets of Monto and found inspiration for his writings, most notably, of course, *Ulysses*.

PENAL
TIMES

In the eighteenth century, Dublin was very similar to other cities in Europe. In the middle of that century it had a population of between 100,000 and 120,000 people, and rapidly expanding with immigration from Britain and rural Ireland. It was regarded in

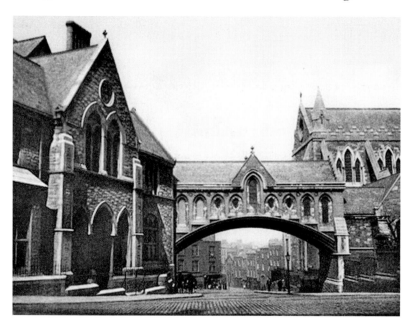

Winetavern Street, *c.* 1900. (Courtesy of GCI)

importance as the second city of the British Empire. The city presented vivid contrasts however, and visitors noted the crowds of beggars, the poor quality of the inns and taverns, the squalid wretchedness of the oldest part, around Christ Church Cathedral, whilst also noting the fine new areas of the city, and the brilliant and hospitable society that lived there. New, fashionable squares and roads were built at the Rutland (now Parnell) Square, Mountjoy and Gardiner Street areas north of the River Liffey, and Stephen's Green, Merrion and Fitzwilliam Squares south of the river. Stephen's Green was boasted of as the largest square in Europe. The Liffey Quays were admired, and the new Irish Parliament House, opposite Trinity College (now Bank of Ireland), built between 1729 and 1739, was regarded with envy. All this prosperity and grandeur was built by the Protestant ascendancy and nobility who ruled Ireland at this time and who were getting ever-more confident, as evidenced by the grandeur of certain parts of Dublin and crowned with the establishment of a separate Irish Parliament (Grattan's Parliament) in the closing decades of the eighteenth century.[1]

THE PENAL LAWS, POVERTY AND MORAL MAYHEM

However, this confidence was based on shaky foundations. There was a price to pay for the improvements in certain parts of Dublin city. According to historian Maurice Craig, 'the dirt, the gaiety, the cruelty, the smells, the pomp, the colour and the sound so remote from anything we know, were all to be found in much the same proportion from Lisbon to St Petersburg.' However, he noted, Dublin was unique because 'it was an extreme example of tendencies generally diffused'. Craig even suggested that Dublin had more in common with Calcutta than European cities. Dublin was, along side its splendour, renowned for its squalor. 'Ireland itself is a poor country, and Dublin a magnificent city; but the appearances of extreme poverty among the lower people are amazing', wrote Benjamin Franklin after a visit to the capital in the early 1770s. The historian W.E.H. Lecky noted that Dublin possessed many elements of disorder, including savage feuds, rioting and bull baiting. The Cornmarket open area near St Audoen's church was the location for bull-baiting, which saw a bull being partially tied to a pole with a rope of a certain length to give it enough space to move and then attacked (or baited) by the fiercest dog possible. The poor of Dublin found this to be of great amusement.[2]

Christ Church Cathedral in the early nineteenth century. It appeared in the *Dublin Saturday Magazine*, Vol. 1, No. 10, 1832.

In 1798, Revd James Whitelaw, rector of St Catherine's church on Thomas Street, described his experience of working in the area of the Liberties, near Christ Church Cathedral: 'the streets are generally narrow; the houses crowded together; numerous lanes and alleys are occupied by working manufacturers, by petty shopkeepers, the labouring poor, and beggars, crowded together to a degree distressing to humanity ...' The tenements which he described as 'truly wretched habitations', often had thirty or forty individuals to a house. Varying degrees of filth and stench, infectious diseases and darkness inconceivable was the life and lot of the wretched inhabitants in the vicinity of the two Dublin cathedrals. He noted the teeming population living in overcrowded conditions and asked, '... why are brothels, soap manufactories, slaughter-houses, glass-houses, lime kiln, distilleries, etc., suffered to exist in such over-crowded conditions?' His Dublin was a place of overwhelming smells, with no decent sewage system, where each house had its own cesspit and where nightsoil-men might empty them every so often. And if they did not, the nearby River Liffey served as a useful cesspit for the inhabitants. His observations were echoed by Curwen, an English visitor, who noted that poverty, disease and wretchedness existed in every great town, but in Dublin he found the misery indescribable.[3]

There are many factors responsible for this chaos. The deplorable state of the poorer classes in the eighteenth century was partially due to the rapid rise in the city's population. In the space of little more than a century the population of Ireland had increased from 1.2 million in 1695 to 6.2 million in 1820, with many rural dwellers fleeing the frequent countryside famines and adding to the chaos and problems of the city. Also, to some extent the curtailment of the Catholic religion may be a significant explanation for the extreme poverty. Because of the Penal Laws (brought into force in 1695 and not repealed until Catholic Emancipation in 1829), the only religion was the established Church. The Penal Laws were, according to Edmund Burke, 'a machine of wise and elaborate contrivance, as well fitted for the oppression, impoverishment and degradation of a people, and the debasement in them of human nature itself, as ever proceeded from the perverted ingenuity of man.' Among other things the laws banned Catholics from owning land, excluded them public office and certain professions and denied them the right to vote.

The result of the laws was that the Protestant planters, in a minority, suddenly became massively wealthy, powerful and privileged, holding the reins of power in the military and government and having the lands, titles and lifestyle to do whatever they wished. They were the new rulers of Ireland, based in Dublin. They were, however, constantly under the scrutiny of London, and all laws pertaining to Ireland first had to be ratified in Britain. Furthermore, with rising prosperity in Ireland as a result of the expansion of the cloth, woollen and linen trades, the UK Government imposed sanctions to ensure that England's economic interests did not suffer.

Street names such as Dirty Lane (now Bridgefoot Street), Mullinahack (from Irish, meaning 'dung hill'), Murdering Lane (off James's Street) and Cow's Lane give an indication of the living conditions in the area around the cathedrals of Dublin. Cutt Throat Lane, also off James's Street, was another name that was somewhat self-explanatory. The lane, which was in existence as far back as 1488, was changed to Roundhead Row in 1876 and Murdering Lane was changed to Cromwell's Quarter, which is still there to this day. It was in this context that the great satirist and wit Jonathan Swift lived. From his vantage point at St Patrick's Cathedral, in the heart of old Dublin, he could plainly see that poor children were living in squalor and wrote about the cruel and inhuman treatment meted out to Ireland by London. *Gulliver's Travels*, *A Modest Proposal* and other writings, tackled the major issues of the day in his unique, satirical style. In *A Modest Proposal*, Swift suggested fattening these undernourished children and then feeding them to the rich people. Children of the poor, he proposed, could be sold into the meat market at the age of one, thus combating Dublin's

Winetavern Street in the early 1960s. (Courtesy of GCI)

rapidly rising population and unemployment. This would spare families the expense of child-rearing while providing them with a little extra income and contributing to the overall economic well-being of the country. Despite such concerns, Swift had little regard for the many beggars of Dublin, whom he regarded as 'thieves, drunkards and whore-mongers'.[4]

Excessive wealth concentrated in the hands of the minority ascendancy created the conditions for excessive poverty for the majority and the consequent adverse social and living conditions. And this is the context for the growth of Hell.

Lanes and alleyways near Winetavern Street, 1960s.
(Courtesy of Dublin Forums/dan1919/breen)

Some charities did exist during this time to try to help the poor of the city. Dublin's oldest charity, the Sick and Indigent Roomkeeper's Society, was founded in 1790 in response to the appalling poverty – the vicinity of the cathedrals. Likewise, the first Dublin Magdalen Asylum was opened in 1765 in an attempt to save prostitutes ('fallen' or 'seduced' women) from a life of vice, debauchery, disease and an untimely death.[5]

THE ORMOND AND LIBERTY BOYS

The 'debasement of human nature', as it was described by Edmund Burke, saw the rise of much violence in the old city, particularly from the 1730s onwards. This was greatly facilitated by having a very poor, almost non-existent, policing (or 'watch') system. A watchman, the forerunner to the policeman, usually carried a bill, which was a long pole with a hook for catching fleeing lawbreakers and a lantern, as public lighting was extremely scarce in old Dublin. However, these watchmen were quite useless when they came up against organised gangs that roamed the city. Gangs such as the Ormond Boys (Catholic butchers from Ormond Quay) and the Liberty Boys (Huguenot Protestant weavers from the Liberties) were constantly at each other's throats – literally, using swords, knives, bludgeons and hangers to slash leg tendons and meat hooks to hang up their victims. This factional fighting, with its bloody battles, reprisals and ferocity, and involving some horrific injuries, lasted throughout the eighteenth century. It often intensified during the many local fair and maypole events.

Duels, kidnappings and murder were also common. One of those murdered was Paul 'Gallows' Farrel, a city constable much hated by the Liberty and Ormond Boys. He was a known informer and the factions joined forces to kidnap, torture and then hang him.[6]

One of the leaders of the Liberty Boys, Thady Foy, murdered a watchman. He was tried and subsequently hanged and quartered outside the Tholsel, at Skinners Row, across from Christ Church Cathedral.

Riots were also frequent and the public whipping of those prosecuted for rioting had little effect. Arguably, all these events were symptoms of a society uncomfortable with the numerous divisions and expressing their discomfort through chaos and violence.[7]

THE PINKING DINDIES

Throughout the eighteenth century, peaking in the 1770s and 1780s, robbery and violence, particularly against women and

Map of Dublin in late eighteenth and early nineteenth centuries showing the area around Hell and the Liberties. (Courtesy of GCI)

prostitutes, were increasingly common for those moving around the city. Chaises and sedans were often pulled over and their occupants held up. Some of the most commonly stolen objects were pocket watches and purses, and silver belt and shoe buckles. It was not uncommon for those walking along the street to be deliberately jostled by a passer-by looking for a duel. Dublin also had swarms of 'sharpers', adept at disguise, shoplifting, pick-pocketing, ring-dropping, coining and availing themselves of any opportunity for procuring money that may arise. Visitors to Dublin were frequently warned to 'look to their pockets' or suffer the consequences.

Another class of thugs (deriving from the ascendancy and essentially Trinity College Dublin students) known as the Pinking Dindies were skilled in the art of 'pinking' – slashing their victims with the point of their protruding swords. A favourite weapon of the students out on a rampage was a heavy metal key attached to an innocuous handkerchief. One would not take too much notice of the handkerchief until one felt the brunt of the key on one's person. Rampant violence in everyday life was an intrinsic part of the character of both the well-off and the dispossessed. The Pinking Dindies were also known as 'rent

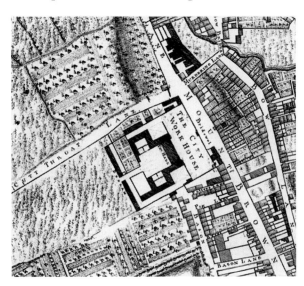

A late eighteenth-century map of Cutt Throat Lane, near the Workhouse for Dublin's poor and destitute. The Workhouse was on the site of present-day James's Street Hospital.

collectors' – essentially racketeers, extorting money from the many prostitutes around the cathedral area.

It was also the time of personalities such as Captain Tiger Roche (b.1729), an army officer notorious for his many crimes and misdemeanours. He lived a life full of action and adventure mixed with violence, including murder, which forced him to flee to America, where he fought in any war he could find. On one occasion when he was arrested for stealing he sank his teeth into a prison guard's throat. On returning to Dublin he challenged the Pinking Dindies on occasion to quell their excesses.

THE MARSHALSEA DEBTOR'S PRISON

Those people who owed money in the eighteenth and nineteenth centuries were quickly confined to the debtor's prison called Marshalsea. Marshalsea Lane was off Thomas Street, between Bridgefoot Street and Watling Street. The lane, formerly beside Lynch's Pub (near Massey's at 141 Thomas Street), is now closed off. It took its name from a group of buildings known as the Marshalsea. The word comes from the name of a court held before the knight marshal of the king to administer justice between the king's servants. The buildings were thought to have been built around 1770. Some of the imposing old walls are still visible from Bonham Street (off Watling Street) and behind the IAWS building on Thomas Street. Marshalsea's debtors from all parts of Ireland were confined with their wives and families. Despite the addition of extra accommodation in the nineteenth century the Marshalsea was always extremely overcrowded while the confined site impeded ventilation. Some of the women in the prison complained at having to share the limited space with prostitutes, 'women of the town, some from the very flags [street walkers]'. The length of a prisoner's stay was determined largely by the whim of their creditors. It was run privately for profit; beds could be rented from the head warder for 1s per night. Those who could not afford a bed were consigned to a damp airless dungeon, about 12ft square and 8ft high, which had no light except that which was admitted through a sewer, which ran close by it and rendered the atmosphere almost insufferable.[8]

THE NUNNERY AND NEWGATE JAIL

Another even more notorious place of confinement was Newgate Gaol at Cornmarket, at the other end of Thomas Street and only a stone's throw from the Four Courts and Hell. Newgate had been one of the entrance gates to the old city wall, situated at the corner of the Cornmarket. It was built of black calp. The remaining section of the old city walls we see today at Cornmarket/Lamb's Alley originally had a tower, which served as a prison in the late Middle Ages. Established as the city gaol by Richard II in 1285, it had four drum towers, one at each corner, with a gate and portcullis. During the Penal Times this jail was full of clerics jailed for their practice of Catholicism. One section of the prison was known as the 'nunnery' because it was used to hold prostitutes who had been captured by the parish watch. It was later used as a debtor's prison.

Its sheer inhumanity reflected the very hard times of the eighteenth century. A contemporary account of the cells for the condemned described them as 'gloomy mansions indeed'. It was a monument of inhumanity and depravity, with the prisoners bound in leg irons all the time and forced to beg outsiders and passers-by for alms and food.

Punishment was particularly vengeful and extreme, reflecting the fears of the wealthy classes over any threats to their cosseted lifestyles. Hangings, burnings, transportation, whippings, pillorying, being placed in the stocks, were the order of the day. People were hanged for stealing, robbing and coining and were often heroes in the eyes of the mob. 'De Night before Larry was

Stretched' and 'The Kilmainham Minuet' (or 'jig') were typical humorous ballads of the 1700s, extolling the good characters of the condemned.

The coffins of those to be executed arrived a few days before their demise, and many of the prisoners sold their bodies to surgeons before their execution. With the money earned, the prisoners would buy much drink and entertain their friends. It was said that many a condemned prisoner used his coffin as a table and for playing cards in the days before his demise.

The Dublin poor were not without diversions or amusements, despite the harsh living conditions they endured. Enormous amounts of pleasure were derived from bull-baiting, cockfighting and attendance at public executions. Between 1780 and 1795, 232 men and 10 women were hanged – such was the violence, mayhem in and the retribution exacted by the city. And this was a city of no more than 140,000 citizens. The prison was demolished in 1839.[9]

Illustration of medieval prostitution in Ireland. (Courtesy of GCI)

In the tumultuous, precarious and dangerous eighteenth century, we find Hell located in the heart of Old Dublin, with its prostitution, taverns, gambling, debauchery, smells, cess-pits and other horrors, and the overall mayhem that was an inevitable product of all the factors outlined above.

A PLACE CALLED HELL: TALES FROM THE CRYPT

Little today remains of the small and narrow gated laneway in front of Dublin's Christ Church Cathedral which bore the arresting name of 'Hell'. The partially arched and gloomy passage was nearly 10ft below the floor level of the cathedral and about 9ft in width. This passage led to the Four Courts and to an open space named Christ Church Yard, about 98ft long by 50ft wide, before the south front of the church and next to Fishamble Street. In the seventeenth century the lane and the adjacent Christ Church Yard became a public thoroughfare, hence their inclusion on Brooking's Map of Dublin for 1728 and Rocque's *Map of Dublin, 1756.* Over time came the name Hell came to refer not just to the laneway but to the wider area around the cathedral that stretched from Cork Hill to Copper Alley, Fishamble Street, Winetavern Street and on to Cook Street, and included the surrounding cobbled lanes and alleyway, in the heart of medieval Dublin – essentially in the shadow of the cathedral and the old walls of the city.

This was where Dublin's and Europe's finest brothels, music halls and theatres, bawdy houses and gambling houses were concentrated, and it was the home to the madam of them all, Darkey Kelly. Hell even had links with the infamous Hellfire Club in the Dublin Mountains. It was a place you entered at your peril – a cauldron of infamy, debauchery, notoriety and murder. Even the authorities were afraid to go near the place. In his book, *Me Jewel and Darlin' Dublin*, Éamonn MacThomáis claimed that the reputation of the area was so bad that The Provost of Trinity College Dublin told the students on more than one occasion that 'Dublin's Hell' was out-of-bounds and that he would expel anyone found there at night-time.[1]

The arch over the iron gate at the entrance to the passage had a large wooden statue of the devil adorning it, greeting the visitor who dared venture into the area at night, a time when the place became even more shadowy because of the dearth of public lighting. This only helped to copper-fasten the area's terrible reputation.

HELL AND ROCQUE'S MAP OF DUBLIN

But did Hell as the stories and legends describe it really exist, or was its reputation a figment of the imagination of locals? What is the truth of the stories that were associated with this part of Dublin for generations? When one looks at maps of Dublin in the seventeenth and eighteenth centuries, the area around Christ Church Cathedral, the oldest part of Dublin, was an area crammed with cramped lanes, alleyways and narrow, sloping streets. There were no wide streets such as we see today. It was a typical, medieval district, with the average street being 12ft wide. Lanes and alleyways were even narrower.

A laneway in the grounds of Christ Church Cathedral was shown on *Brookings Map of Dublin* for 1728 and named 'Hell' on Rocque's *Map of Dublin, 1756*. Rocque's map shows the name and location of Hell, so there is absolutely no doubt as to its existence and exact location. It was a narrow, winding alleyway or passage beginning at the corner of Christ Church Lane (later renamed St Michael's Hill) and Skinners Row (later Christ Church Place). This lane led to the old Four Courts and Christ Church

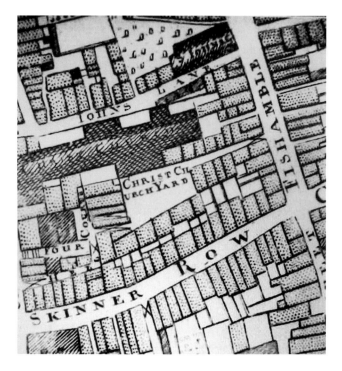

Excerpt from Rocque's *Map of Dublin, 1756* showing the Location of Hell at junction of Skinners Row (Christ Church Place) and Christ Church Lane (St Michael's Hill) and in the grounds of Christ Church Cathedral. (Courtesy of UCD Library/Harvard University/Dublin City Libraries Archive)

Yard – both in the grounds at the front of the cathedral, facing south. The Courts and the Yard were also accessible via the same lane from Fishamble Street, near Copper Alley. Leonard Strangeways' 1904 map, 'The Walls of Dublin (from all available authorities)' includes the Devil's Head and shows its precise location at the Fishamble Street entrance to the alleyway called Hell.

Further evidence of the existence of Hell come from surviving eighteenth-century newspaper advertisements offered lettings of furnished apartments in Hell. In fact, the earliest surviving advertisement for such lodgings was in the *Universal Adventurer* of 11 November 1753. Nearby at the junction with High Street and Christ Church Lane was meeting place of 'loungers' from various classes, and the location was called 'Idler's Corner'.[2]

TALES FROM THE CRYPT

Beside and overlooking Winetavern Street we have Christ Church Cathedral. Dublin has two cathedrals, Christ Church and St Patrick's, which, following the sixteenth-century Reformation both became part of the Established Church of Henry VIII. Consequently, there were no Catholic cathedrals and few churches in the city until the church-building era after the granting of Catholic Emancipation in 1829. In 1172 Dublin's first archbishop, Laurence O'Toole, replaced the original wooden Christ Church Cathedral with the stone Romanesque building we see today.

Inside the cathedral one finds steps leading down to a huge crypt, running the whole length of the building. The present entrance was not always there; for centuries the main entrance to this vast underground area was from outside, not inside, the church, and this important feature was to have a major influence on its use. The external entrances to this crypt were from

The east end of the crypt of Christ Church as drawn by H.W. Brewer in 1882.

the cloister in front of the cathedral, via Hell's Lane, and from St John's Lane East at the back.[3]

The cathedral's crypt is enormous with vaulted ceilings and shadowy caverns. It has essentially been the same for the past 1,000 years. It dates from the twelfth, possibly even eleventh, century, and is not only one of the largest medieval crypts in the UK and Ireland, but also the oldest structure in Dublin. It is a forest of heavy rough-stone pillars, which carries the weight of the cathedral and central tower.

Crypts were traditionally used for burials, contained chapels or held relics, but it would appear that in the case of Christ Church Cathedral this was not the custom. It is not quite clear what it was used for initially, but it is reported from as far back as the fourteenth century that it was used as a warehouse to store French wine.[4] In the seventeenth century it was divided up and rented out as shops and taverns. Its size and shape would have greatly facilitated this. By 1740 there were already shops and stalls in the precincts of the cathedral and though 'tippling houses' had once been banned, taverns had sprung up, below and around the cathedral, and it was reported that 'the Lord's Day is profaned, and the neighbours inconvenienced' by the several tavern-owners who were licensed to trade in alcohol. By this time, many of the church buildings surrounding the cathedral that had formerly had religious functions had been secularised, and the cathedral itself needed urgent remedial work. Other activities undertaken in the precincts of the cathedral included the making of musical instruments, music publishing, legal practice, hawking and various trades ranging from candle-making to leather-working. Strongbow's Tomb was frequently used as the site for agreeing rents and leases.[5]

HEAVEN AND HELL:
SPIRITS DIVINE AND SPIRITS OF WINE

Since the Middle Ages St John's Lane East, extending from Fishamble Street at the immediate north-facing back of the cathedral to Winetavern Street and what was known as Cock Hill, had been mainly occupied by wine taverns and vintners' cellars, many of which were described as located under Christ Church Cathedral. By the sixteenth century, such was the extent of profits from a thriving business in ales, whiskey and wines, that the owners of other taverns nearby had gradually moved into the crypt of the cathedral and set up business. In 1548, the cathedral leased to Arlan Ussher, merchant, the 'wine-tavern under the said church, which the said Arland then enjoyed'. In 1594 another wine tavern under the cathedral was leased to Richard Ussher. In 1626 there were many other taverns in the vicinity with names such as the 'Dragon' cellar, the 'Redd Stagge' cellar, the 'Redd Lyon' cellar, and the 'Starr' cellar.

In a letter from Dublin Castle in 1633, the Lord Deputy Wentworth complained to the Archbishop of Canterbury about the cellars and taverns under the cathedral: '[the] vaults underneath the church itself turned all to ale houses and tobacco shops, where they are pouring either in or out their drink offerings and incense, whilst we above are serving the high God'.[6]

In 1629, according to historian John Gilbert, we find here the 'Shipp' cellar and house, the 'Half Moon' cellar and, significantly, the 'cellar called Hell'. So it would appear that the lane and the wider area may have derived its name from the Hell tavern located in the crypt of Christ Church Cathedral. But why was the tavern called Hell? There are several stories giving possible explanations. One story relates to a crypt-keeper who locked up the tavern for the winter months and inadvertently left behind a customer who spent the winter there in the freezing cold. On reopening for business the following spring, the crypt-keeper found the customer still there – but now a skeleton! When the story spread, it might have been the reason locals called the tavern Hell.

During excavations in the late nineteenth century, archaeologists discovered a small store of ancient liquor bottles, one still containing liquid. According to an archaeologist, 'a glass of it was tried on a too-willing bystander, with the effect that he will probably never desire to try unknown liquors again in his lifetime.' Experts at the Guinness brewery pronounced it to be the decomposed remains of a malt liquor.

Another story connected to the name of the lane, Hell, tells of how some of the judges and barristers in the nearby Four Courts used to work and live in the area, thereby making the locals feel somewhat nervous. Not only that, but the frequent heavy sentences passed on some of the poor unfortunates, resonated with people and over time the area became known as Hell. In fact, such was the horror, fear and dread associated with the courts here that it was not unknown for the condemned defendant,

The crypt of Christ Church Cathedral, where there was once a tavern called Hell.

Environs of Hell. The cathedral from the south, as shown in a lithograph in
R. O'Callaghan Newenham's *Picturesque Views of the Antiquities of Ireland*, 1826.

waiting to be sentenced, to drop dead out of sheer fright at the
thought of being sentenced to the 'Hell's Hornpipe' or the 'Devil's
Drop', as hanging was often called when the sentence was meted
out from here.

A visitor to Christ Church Cathedral in the 1760s, George Street,
noted that 'to the south of the chapter house was another narrow
chamber [passage] which in these days has come to be popularly called Hell, probably on account of a grotesque figure
preserved there.'

Whatever the origin of the name, such was the mayhem and
madness in the area, combined with the unique Liberties humour
in acknowledging the irony of the location of a tavern in the crypt
beneath the hallowed walls of Christ Church Cathedral, ensured
that the name Hell was appropriate and thus it stuck. A wit of the
day commented:

Rear of Christ Church Cathedral from Winetavern Street in the late 1940s.
(Courtesy of GCI)

> Spirits above and spirits below,
> Spirits divine and spirits – of wine.[7]

However, the Earl of Wentworth decided to take action about the carousing going on in the crypt 'whilst we above are serving the high God'. He ordered, 'for the redress of sundry abuses', the removal of the taverns and issued an ordinance decreeing, amongst other things, 'that no person presume to make urine against the walls of the said church'.[8]

Wentworth's action had a short-lived effect, however, and the commercial life of Dublin continued under and around the cathedral for many years afterwards, with shops, taverns and businesses, courts, brothels and bawdy houses all jostling for position and opportunity.

IN THE SHADOW OF THE CATHEDRAL:
THE FOUR COURTS AND HELL

Space was much in demand in the old Dublin of the eighteenth century. Unlike today, Christ Church Cathedral was closely hemmed in on all sides from the medieval period onwards, surrounded by a warren of narrow lanes and alleyways. Gates were a feature of many of these lanes. For example, gates at Fishamble Street and Christ Church Lane led through to the grounds of the cathedral. In the grounds of the cathedral stood the old Four Courts, described by a contemporary as 'a miserable collection of closets in a dark dirty hall'.[9]

One of the entrances to Hell was behind the trees and shrubs in the grounds of Christ Church Cathedral. Today, a gate marks this entrance. (Courtesy of Fotofinish)

The old Four Courts was so called because of the Four Courts of justice under the English legal system operating in the Pale. Outside the confines of the Pale the ancient Irish legal system, Brehon Law, operated for centuries. This was (and still is) widely regarded as a far more equitable and distinctly advanced legal system in its dealings with both men and women. In 1606 the Four Courts (also 'the King's Courts') moved across the river for a short time, but due to pressure from Dublin Corporation, which wanted to keep it within the confines of the old city, the courts moved back across the River Liffey in 1608 to a new home in the grounds of Christ Church Cathedral and the adjoining Christ Church Place. The entrance hall of the courts was long and narrow, crowned by an octangular cupola. According to Frank Hopkins in his book *Hidden Dublin*, those entering the Four Courts walked through 'Hell', under the Devil's head adorning the arched and

The Four Courts in their present location. Old Four Courts were on the south side of the River Liffey in the grounds of Christ Church Cathedral. (Courtesy of Dublin Forums)

gloomy entrance. This would not have been any comfort to those facing trial. To the left of the door, steps led to the Court of Exchequer, to the right was the Chancellor's Court, next to which was the Court of Common Pleas, while the King's Bench was placed opposite the Court of Exchequer – hence the name the Four Courts.

It was the venue for one of the longest trials in the eighteenth century – the case of James Annesley against the Earl of Anglesey that took place in late 1743. This renowned case involved skulduggery, kidnapping, white slavery and attempted murder, and captured the imaginations of many in Ireland and England at the time with Annesley claiming he had been robbed of his rightful inheritance by the Earl. The final verdict went in James's favour and his estates were returned to him, but he did not obtain his titles before he died at the age of 44. This infamous case was the inspiration for Walter Scott's novel *Guy Mannering* and Robert Louis Stevenson's 1888 novel, *Kidnapped*.[10]

By the latter half of the eighteenth century the tone of area around Hell and the Four Courts had deteriorated. Almost all the Cathedral buildings were rented out, along with their basements. Most available space was rented for shops, houses, courts, lawyers' rooms, and taverns or 'tippling houses'. Essentially, the legal and commercial life of the old city mingled, extending around and under the cathedral and bursting out through the crypt along St John's Lane, where there were more huckster shop displaying their wares against the back walls of the cathedral. The area had become a rabbit warren of lanes, alleyways with tawdry cage work structures involved in legal and illegal activity – the oldest and second oldest professions in the world making strange yet comfortable bed-fellows. The greatest concentration of brothels and bawdy houses in Dublin were in this area.[11]

By the end of the eighteenth century the space proved inadequate and the offices of the courts and the legal records remained dispersed. Added to which, many of the Four Courts buildings were in a dilapidated condition. A decision was therefore made to build a new structure on the present site across the River Liffey. The new buildings were designed by Thomas Cooley and James Gandon and work began in 1775. However, it was not until the very end of the eighteenth century that the Four Courts moved from the vicinity of Christ Church Cathedral to its present location at Inns Quay, still facing south and overlooking the River Liffey.

Interestingly, it is still possible today to follow the former lane, called Hell, along a path through the railed front area of the cathedral. The present entrance is a gate near the arch at St Michael's Hill. There are a number of steps down to the path, which then winds its way past the old ruins in the grounds and leads to the exit that is also a gate facing on to Fishamble Street.

Winetavern Street early twentieth century. (Courtesy of GCI)

WALKING THROUGH HELL'S GATES

Philip Dixon Hardy, in a letter to the editor of the *Dublin Penny Journal*, in 1832 described his experience of walking through Hell on his way to the old Four Courts at the front of Christ Church Cathedral:

> I remember, instead of turning to the right down Parliament-street, going, in my youth, straightforward under the Exchange and up Cork-hill, to the old Four Courts, adjoining Christ Church cathedral. I remember what an immense crowd of cars, carriages, noddies, and sedan chairs beset our way as we struggled on between Latouche's and Gleadowe's Banks in Castle-street – what a labour it was to urge on our way through Skinner-row – I remember looking up to the old cage-work wooden house that stood at the corner of Castle-street and Werburgh-street, and wondering why, as it overhung so much, it did not fall down – and then turning down Fishamble-street, and approaching the Four Courts, that then existed, through what properly was denominated Christ Church Yard, but which popularly was called Hell.
>
> This was certainly a very profane and unseemly soubriquet, to give to a place that adjoined a Cathedral whose name was Christ Church; and my young mind, when I first entered there, was struck with its unseemliness. Yes; and more especially, when over the arched entrance there was pointed out to me the very image of the devil, carved in oak, and not unlike one of those hideous black figures that are still in Thomas-street, hung over Tobacconists' doors.
>
> This locale of Hell, and this representation of his satanic majesty, was famous in those days even beyond the walls of Dublin. I remember well, on returning to my native town after my first visit to Dublin, being asked by all my playfellows, had I been in Hell, and had I seen the devil.
>
> Its fame even reached Scotland, and Burns the Poet, (1759-1796) in his story of 'Death and Doctor Hornbook', (which tells of a drunken narrator's late night encounter with Death), alludes to this part of Dublin when he writes:

But this that I am gean to tell,
Which lately on a night befell
Is just as true as the Deil's in Hell,
Or Dublin city.

As Hell has not now any local habitation in our city, neither has the devil – but I can assure you, reader, that there are relics preserved of this very statue to this day; some of it was made into much esteemed snuff-boxes – and I am told there is one antiquarian in our city, who possesses the head and horns, and who prizes the relic as the most valuable in his museum. At any rate, Hell to me, in those days, was a most attractive place, and often did I go hither, for the yard was full of shops where toys, and fireworks, and kites, and all the playthings that engage the youthful fancy, were exposed for sale. But Hell was not only attractive to little boys, but also to bearded men: for here were comfortable lodgings for single men, and I remember reading in a journal of the day, an advertisement, intimating that there were

Christ Church Cathedral from the air in the mid-twentieth century. The lane called Hell is visible to the south of cathedral, running from St Michael's Hill to Fishamble Street. (Courtesy of GCI)

Shopping in one of the many second-hand clothes shops on Winetavern Street in the late 1940s. (Courtesy of Dublin Forums)

'To be let, furnished apartments in Hell. N.B. They are well suited to a lawyer'.[12]

Hardy continued:

Here also were sundry taverns and snuggeries, where the counsellor would cosher with the attorney – where the prebendary and the canon

45

of the cathedral could meet and make merry – here the old stagers, the seniors of the Currans, the Yelvertons, and the Bully Egans, would enjoy the concomitants of good fellowship … and cracked their jokes and their marrow-bones, toasted away claret, and tossed repartee, until they died, as other men die and are forgotten.[13]

THE FORTY STEPS TO HELL

Beside the two St Audoen's churches on Dublin's High Street we have the famous Forty Steps to Hell – the stepped passageway linking High Street to the Cook Street part of the area known as Hell, a short distance from the cathedral.

The entrance to the steps is from St Audoen's Park, and here one is able to walk the old battlements of the ancient walls of the medieval city of Dublin. One also sees the doorway and belfry of the church (Church of Ireland), as it is the only surviving medieval church within the walls of the city. The tower loft contains the six bells, three of which have been in use since 1423 (except for the period 1898–1983) and are thus claimed to be the oldest still-used church bells in Dublin. The bells also rang out at curfew time and in times of communal danger. The tenor was tolled each evening at 8 p.m. and was known locally as 'the old cow'. The present clock came from St Peter's church, Aungier Street, after that church was demolished in the early 1980s. The now blocked Foundling's Door of St Audoen's tells the story of how impoverished women of Hell would leave their babies in a basket in the door which revolved inwards. The children were then placed in orphanages by the Church.[1]

Between the back of the church and the official entrance to the church, there is the Lucky Stone perched up against a wall in a

St Audoen's church on High Street and the gateway leading to Forty Steps to Hell. (Courtesy of GCI)

cell-like circular passageway. This is a late ninth-century grave slab adorned with a Greek-style cross. It stood outside the tower of St Audoen's for centuries. It was regarded as being the source of luck for many local business for generations and many were seen touching the stone in the mornings prior to engaging in their daily business.[2]

Standing in the park, you are at the original height of the battlements, from which Norman invaders would have defended the city from the likes of Silken Thomas and other disaffected Irish from beyond the Pale. If you walk through the arch and down the steps you will be able to see the old stones making up the wall and which were part of the original St Columcille's church which stood on this site in the seventh century. There is a real medieval atmosphere and sensation about this place. The back of the Catholic church of St Audoen building looks quite grim and overpowering when viewed from Cook Street, where it seems to tower endlessly above the old city wall and this part of the old area called Hell.[3]

The Forty Steps to Hell at the side of St Audoen's church. (Courtesy of Irish Central)

The narrow passageway and the Forty Steps to Hell along the side of the church lead to a view of the impressive old city wall and a thirteenth-century gate (1240), St Audoen's Arch (also known as Hell's Gate), the only remaining gateway into the old medieval walled city. On the way down there is another, smaller archway at the rear of St Audoen's church, where once a medieval passage led down to the River Liffey. Remains of this passageway have been preserved and may be viewed inside the church.

IN THE SHADOW OF THE OLD WALLS OF DUBLIN

The Forty Steps to Hell lead to Cook Street. This street, at the base of the city wall, was first built in the thirteenth century (the earliest mention of it is in 1270), and it was so named because of the concentration of food vendors, whose ovens were placed outside the walls to reduce the risk of fire, particularly because Dublin was a city constructed largely of wood. The Guild of Cooks had their Guild Hall in this street. Other areas in the Liberties still have names which describe the ancient trades carried on there, including Cornmarket, Winetavern Street, Weaver's Square, Golden Lane, Copper Alley and Fishamble Street.[4]

Cook Street was later famous as it was the hub of the printing industry. In 1571 the first book in Irish was printed here. It was home to several Catholic stationers and printers in the eighteenth century, and the first copy of the *Freeman's Journal* came off the printing press here in 1763.

From 1770, a tavern called the 'Struggler' was located along the street and became the meeting place for members of the Society of United Irishmen. The sign from which the tavern acquired its name showed a man struggling to maintain his position upon a terrestrial globe. A competing tavern called the 'New Struggler' opened a few years later at the opposite end

Going from Hell to Heaven – 1950s image of the steep hill from Cook Street and up to Augustine Street at side of John's Lane church, Thomas Street. (Courtesy of Dublin Forums/nansson)

of the street and was for many years one of the most popular taverns in the area.

Swan Alley, off Cook Street, was another disreputable area full of gambling dens and unsavoury individuals. One such person was George Hendrick, known as the 'Crazy Crow' because of his eccentric and dangerous lifestyle. Despite repeated efforts by the City Fathers to close the gambling houses they just re-opened under a new guise. Swan Alley did much to add to the enduring reputation of Hell.[5]

Keyser's Lane, which led from Cook Street up the steep hill to Cornmarket, was popularly known by locals as 'Kiss-Arse' Lane.

Black Dog Prison, Cornmarket. From the early eighteenth century the Black Dog functioned as the main debtors' prison in Dublin. One section of the prison was called the 'nunnery' because it was used to hold prostitutes who had been captured by the parish watch. It closed as a prison in 1794. (Courtesy of Archiseek)

As with many of the lanes and alleyways in the Hell area connecting to Cook and Winetavern Streets, Keyser's Lane was a very steep and narrow lane. According to historian John Gilbert, it was described in 1587 as 'steepe and slipperie, in which otherwhiles, they that make more haste than good speed clinke their backs to the stones'.

HELL'S COFFIN COLONY

Because it was in the vicinity of Hell, the Four Courts and Newgate, Cook Street was unsurprisingly a profitable location for coffin makers. It was once described as a 'coffin colony'. Coffins came into general use in Dublin towards the end of the seventeenth century. Previously people had been buried in shrouds. From 1850 onwards many coffin makers had their businesses here, opening shroud warehouses and displaying their wares in large open sheds that also housed the hearses. Thomas Roper, operating from the Sign of the Coffin, supplied 'plain oak coffins neatly furnished' or a more elaborate 'fully mounted coffin, silvered, lined and coated'. At one time there were twenty-five undertakers in Dublin, of whom nineteen lived in this street. They used to say that it was the only place in Dublin where you could buy a second-hand coffin – that didn't mean that it had been down and back up again, but that it was shop soiled.[6]

WINETAVERN STREET
AND SMOCK ALLEY

Cook Street leads us to Winetavern Street. The story of Hell particularly involves Winetavern Street, as it lies in the shadow of Christ Church Cathedral, at the very heart of medieval Dublin, and its activities had a direct bearing on the role of the cathedral crypt. Running along the west side of Christ Church Cathedral and descending to the River Liffey under the famous arch, this street was cobblestoned until the late twentieth century. For many years there were several quaint shops and squalid, dingy alleys and lanes adjacent to the street. In latter centuries it became a street of tall, crooked houses. Dublin's narrowest house and smallest shop occupied a site here for many years.

There were numerous taverns along its sloping route from early medieval times, hence the name of this famous thorough-fare. In medieval times the keepers were described as 'taverners'. In 1185 the Abbey of Thomas Court was granted a tax from ale and mead sold in the local taverns. The Archbishop of Dublin in the twelfth century, Laurence O'Toole, based in the nearby Christ Church Cathedral, used to entertain his guests with various kinds of wine bought from these taverns. In the reign of Elizabeth I, Lord Mountjoy reported that French and Spanish wines were sold, though the merchants more commonly sold them by pints and quarts in their own cellars. He noted that when the native

The Irish House in the 1930s. This was one of the last of the many taverns that were on Winetavern Street and environs. Some of the sculpture and plasterwork that adorned this unique building is to be found today in the Dublin Civic Trust in Castle Street. (Courtesy of Dublin Forums/Ditto/Pat Comerford/DCT)

Irish went to the market to sell a cow or a horse, they never returned home until they had drunk the price in Spanish wine, 'which they call the King of Spain's Daughter'.[1]

Many of the 137 taverns, alehouses and cellars in Winetavern Street in the early part of the sixteenth century were listed in the rentals of the property of the cathedral. It was well known that in Dublin wine was half the price it was in London and was sold at double the rate. Such was the popularity of the taverns that, according to Barnaby Rych, an English soldier and author writing on the taverns in the early seventeenth century, the mayor and aldermen 'winked at' and 'tolerated' the 'multitude of alehouses' that were the 'nurseries of drunkenness' and 'all manner of idleness', of 'whoredom and many other vile abominations'. He noted that 'every filthy alehouse has a number of young, idle housewives that are very loathsome, filthy and abominable, both in life and manners, and these they call tavern-keepers, the most of them known as harlots.' In 1677 Dublin was described by Revd Francis O'Molloy as the city 'of the wine flasks'. In the reign of Charles II there were 1,180 alehouses and ninety-one brew-houses in the city. Popular taverns in Winetavern Street included, the 'Black Boy Cellar', the 'Golden Lyon', the 'Common Cellar', the 'Spread Eagle' the 'King's Head', and the 'Golden Dragon'.

Winetavern Street. *c.* 1940. (Courtesy of GCI)

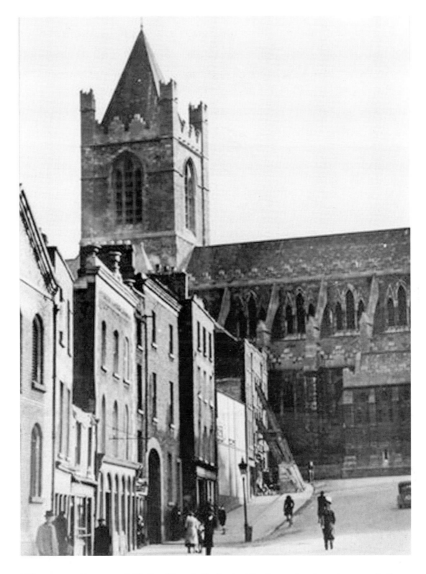

Winetavern Street and Christ Church Cathedral in the 1950s, twenty years before demolition of houses for the building of Wood Quay office blocks. (Courtesy of GCI)

The sheer number of 'dram shops' in Dublin licensed to sell spirits caught the attention of visitors. By the middle of the eighteenth century there were 2,000 alehouses, 300 taverns, and 1,200 brandy shops in the city. In the Winetavern Street area, the number of alehouses formed one fifth of the total number of buildings. The immoderate drinking seems to have really taken off in the 1740s. It was not just the wretchedness of living conditions, the fact life was cheap and short, and the preference for ale over water that stimulated this upsurge in drinking. Low excise duties were also a factor. The government fostered the distilling industry in the city because of the revenue it brought in. In 1788 the High Sheriff of Dublin petitioned Parliament that the drinking of liquor had risen among the lower ranks of the people to such an alarming degree that it occasioned the loss of health of many, debauched the morals of the people and encouraged them into the most shocking excesses of riot and vice.[2]

The Guild of Tailors had its rooms in the street, and Dublin's oldest candlemaker, Rathborne's, was located here from the Middle Ages well into the twentieth century, before it moved to East Wall.

The celebrated row of houses on St Michael's Hill and Winetavern Street, seen in old images of the area, each with a

St Michael's Lane in Hell in the late nineteenth century. (Courtesy of GCI)

single, large tripartite window at first- and second-floor levels, dated from *c*. 1800. The entire block, which extended down the hill to Cook Street and backed onto St Michael's Lane, was occupied by generations of 'clothes brokers' or second-hand clothes dealers, by pawnbrokers and O'Reilly's Auction Rooms. One of Dublin's most famous pawnbrokers, known far and wide as 'the Bicycle Pawn Office', was located here.

St Michael's Hill was originally called Christ Church Lane to which there was a reference in 1354. The name changed to its present form in the early nineteenth century and came from its proximity to the church of St Michael, the tower of which survives in the Synod Hall today.[3]

THE LIBERATOR, THE FREEDOM BELL AND SMOCK ALLEY

Just off Winetavern Street we have the old Smock Alley Theatre. It derived its name from its location on Smock Alley. Such was the notoriety of the alley, with gambling houses, taverns and brothels, that the authorities tried to expunge its reputation by renaming it, first as Orange Street, and later, in 1839, as Essex Street West. This street was named after the Viceroy, Arthur Capel, Earl of Essex who was Irish Lord Lieutenant from 1672 to 77, and who, significantly, was acquainted with members of the Temple family who owned much land in the area. Despite the change, the name Smock Alley endured among the locals.

The theatre opened to the public in 1662 as Dublin's first purpose-built theatre and remains today very much the same as when it was built. The building is consequently a very important site in the history of European theatre. Amongst the playwrights that contributed to its success were Oliver Goldsmith, Richard Brinsley Sheridan and George Farquhar. The latter was accidentally stabbed on stage on one occasion! The much revered actor of the eighteenth century, David Garrick, played Hamlet here in 1741. But the theatre also attracted prostitutes to the area and consolidated the district as a place of vice. Indeed, the public sometimes saw little difference between actresses and prostitutes. Whatever the truth of this, the locale around the theatre saw the growing numbers of bawdy houses during its existence.[4]

The theatre closed in 1787 and subsequently became a Catholic church. When the bell rang in 1811, it was the first Catholic church bell rung in Dublin in nearly 300 years. Dublin's 'freedom bell', as it was later called, rang out in breach of the Penal Laws. Fr Blake, the priest involved, faced charges for his defiance, but was successfully defended by Daniel O'Connell, The Liberator. Legend has it that O'Connell, Lord Mayor at the time, subsequently rang the bell to celebrate the granting of Catholic Emancipation in 1829, creating the crack which remains visible today. With the movement of population from the city confines to the growing suburbs in the twentieth century, the church's usefulness as a place of worship waned and it was subsequently deconsecrated and sold, but with the proviso that the freedom bell, stained-glass windows, ornate ceiling plasterwork and the essential structure remain in situ. The new owners, however, had not forgotten the buildings earlier illustrious career and re-opened it as the Smock Alley Theatre.

Smock Alley itself (i.e. the alley), in keeping with its dubious reputation, witnessed serious riots in 1768, with the destruction of much property and loss of life. The riots followed the murder of a butcher by some of the corrupt characters who frequented the disreputable network of gambling houses and brothels in the area. The mob attacked and wrecked the establishments they suspected the villains were hiding in. These included Madden's, The Globe, Reilly's Tavern, Ben Johnson's Head and many brothels.

Gambling houses of the worst type flourished in the Smock Alley area during the eighteenth century. One renowned and disreputable gambler was known as Mendoza. He and his gang used false dice at the 'stamps' or 'hazard-tables'. In a police raid in 1790, as well as a number of these false dice, the skeleton of a man who had fallen victim to Mendoza and his gang was found in a cellar.[5]

Famous taverns in the area included the Bull's Head, the Unicorn and the Elephant. According to historian Donal Fallon:

> The latter took its name from a rather bizarre incident in the history of the city. On 17 June 1681, an elephant which had been taken to Dublin for display at an exhibition met a tragic end when the stable he was being kept in at Essex Street caught fire. This spectacle brought huge crowds onto the street, and when the fire was extinguished they proceeded to take parts of the elephant away as souvenirs.

The Elephant tavern appears to have served as a meeting place for the first Catholic Committee in the 1760s, a forerunner of the influential Catholic Association of Daniel O'Connell in the nineteenth century.[6]

BLIND PETER AND BLIND QUAY

Also located on Essex Street was The Globe, which has been described by the Dublin historian J.T. Gilbert as one of the most important taverns of the period. He notes that 'this house was the chief resort of the Dublin politicians during the reign of George II', and that it attracted 'merchants, physicians, and lawyers', among others. An interesting character by the name of 'Blind Peter', famed for his wit, comes up in many accounts of this pub. A shoe black (polisher), he was described in one publication as 'of hideous aspect, he had but one eye, was most inveterately pitted with the same pox, and his face completely tattooed with the scars he received in the various battles he had fought'.[7]

The Bear Tavern was kept by a man named David Corbet until his death in 1787, and he was described by J.T. Gilbert as a Freemason, as well as 'an excellent musician, and leader of the band of the Dublin Independent Volunteers'. Several taverns in the area spent some time in Huguenot hands in the late seventeenth and early eighteenth centuries, such as the Three Tuns on Blind Quay, today known to us as Exchange Street. This pub was owned by Jean Chaigneau, a merchant who purchased the building for £200 in the 1720s. Ruben's Head and the Two Friends Tavern, just off Crow Street, were also owned

Fishamble Street in the 1970s. The building work for Wood Quay office blocks is behind the wooden hoarding. (Courtesy of Fotofinish)

by members of the Huguenot community. J.T. Gilbert listed a host of other local taverns in his work, including the Raven and Punch Bowl, which he dated to 1729, and the Dog and Duck, which was said to be 'noted for good ale', and the Turk's Head Chop House, which he dates to the 1760s (the name is still in use today).

On Exchange Street Lower it is still possible to see the ruins of Isolde's Tower, one of Dublin's hidden treasures. According to Nordic legend, Isolde was an Irish princess who was supposed to marry a Cornish nobleman, Prince Mark, but after taking a love potion instead fell in love with a knight named Tristan, who was bringing her across the Irish Sea to England. Their tragic love story ended with both drinking a poisonous concoction. The story was the inspiration for Wagner's opera *Tristan and Isolde*[8] and the legend gave its name to Isolde's Tower, a thirteenth-century tower that was part of the old city walls of Dublin.

Environs of Hell. The exterior of the cathedral from the west showing Winetavern Street and St Michael's Hill. Scene from a drawing by George Petrie, engraved in R. Cromwell's *Excursions through Ireland*, 1820.

In 1993, when digging up the foundations for the new apartment block above, archaeologists found a substantial part of the original Isolde's Tower. The foundations of the old city wall were also visible, continuing from two sides of the surviving lower part of the original tower. It was estimated that the tower stood at nearly 40ft before it was demolished in the seventeenth century. The tower's remains were incorporated into the new building and are now partly visible behind an iron gate.

COPPER ALLEY AND FISHAMBLE STREET

Between Essex Street and the Wood Quay offices, we have Copper Alley – Dublin's oldest medieval street – and Fishamble Street. A shamble was a booth or stall from which goods, in this case fish, were sold. This small area was once

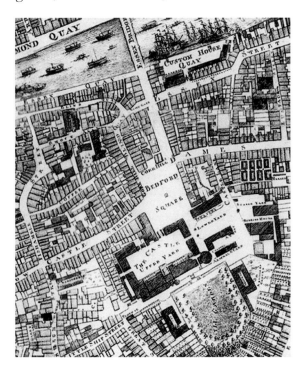

Map showing Fishamble Street, Smock Alley, Copper Alley, Cork Hill and Custom House Quay near the area called Hell in the late eighteenth century. (Courtesy of GCI)

the centre of commercial life in Dublin, with the old Custom House located nearby at Essex Bridge. It was therefore a hive of activity, with fishmongers, sailors, printers, publishers, prostitutes, lawyers, taverners, candle-makers, leatherworkers and many other trades all jostling together in a very small area. Fishamble Street leads down to the River Liffey Quays, at that time Dublin's docks, where fishermen would have off-loaded their catch to the fish hawkers who had their shambles nearby. As such the area would have been prey to the many vices that inevitably flourish at a busy port.

Fishamble Street was the location of the Bull's Head tavern. This was a very popular tavern in Dublin and it was here that the Bull's Head Society, a charitable music group, used to meet every Friday evening. Some of the choir of St Patrick's Cathedral

Sketch of Fishamble Street. (Courtesy of Dublin Forums)

used to participate in musical events in the tavern. Jonathan Swift (writer of *Gulliver's Travels* and Dean of the cathedral 1715–45), however, was not happy with reports of members of the choir consorting with fiddlers in the tavern and quickly condemned the practice. His distaste was hardly surprising; many of the area's taverns were foul dens, devoted to the pleasures of the sailors, the poor, the gamblers, the drinkers and those seeking debauchery. The Grand Order of Masons (the Irish Freemasons) also used the tavern as a venue. Other taverns in Fishamble Street included the Swan Tavern, Ormond's Arms, the Ossory, the Fleece Tavern, the Bear Tavern (in Christ Church Yard) and the London Tavern.

During this period the musical society opened its new music hall on Fishamble Street. In 1742 Handel's *Messiah* was first performed here; in the course of the musicians' stay in

One of Dublin's oldest houses, No. 25 Fishamble Street at the corner of Essex Street.

Dublin a passage was opened from Copper Alley to allow access to the music hall. The first masquerade ball held in Ireland also took place here, on 19 April 1776. However, in 1780 the first Irish State Lottery was drawn in the music hall, thereby adding further to the gambling frenzy of the area.

On the corner of Fishamble Street and Essex Street is no. 26 Fishamble Street, a picturesque and architecturally significant old house both internally and externally. This listed house was built in the 1720s and consists of nearly twenty rooms and many windows. The house has been in the same family for close to 250 years.

THE MOLL MALONE

According to Dublin folklore, one interesting resident who lived, died and had her funeral in and near Fishamble Street was the fishmonger's daughter Molly Malone, who, according to the ballad, 'wheeled her wheelbarrow through streets broad and narrow, crying "cockles and mussels, alive, alive o!"' Her parents ran a fishmongering business at one of the fish shambles on the street and resided nearby. She died at the young age of 36, having succumbed to one of the diseases that pervaded the area from time to time. Her funeral was held in the church of St John, Fishamble Street, and she was buried in the adjacent graveyard. Her legend lives on and the ballad is Dublin's unofficial anthem.

The part of the legend surrounding Molly Malone that has been forgotten or ignored was that she worked part-time in the evenings and nights as a prostitute. This is not very surprising considering that where she grew up and lived was part of the notorious Hell. Moreover, one interpretation of her name, 'Molly' is that it derived from 'moll', the slang word for prostitute. Her statue adorns St Andrew's Street today, commissioned by Dublin Corporation, and her provocative attire gives some credence to this

Fishamble Street in the heart of Hell. The entrance to the Music Hall, where renowned composer Handel introduced the world to his composition *The Messiah*, was under the arch, with No. 19, the former premises of Kennan & Sons, beside it to the right.

aspect of the legend. This statue is known colloquially as 'The Tart with the Cart', 'The Disk with the Fish', 'The Trollop with the Scallops', 'The Dolly with the Trolley', and 'The Flirt with the Skirt'. It portrays Molly as a busty young woman in late eighteenth-century dress.

Interestingly, a late eighteenth-century book containing the earliest known version of 'Molly Malone' reinforces this view of the iconic heroine. Lyrics found in the antique book suggest that Molly was not the virtuous, tragic girl who merely sold cockles and mussels, as we are told in the popular ballad we hear today. A copy of *Apollo's Medley*, published in Doncaster, England, around 1791 and rediscovered in 2010, contains a song referring to 'Sweet Molly Malone' and ends with the lines:

Och! I'll roar and I'll groan,
My sweet Molly Malone,
Till I'm bone of your bone,
And asleep in your bed.
Sweet Molly, Sweet Molly Malone,
Sweet Molly, Sweet Molly Malone.

Despite this, the folklore continues in Dublin that Molly was merely a pretty young fishmonger and that her ghost still haunts Dublin crying 'Cockles and mussels, alive, alive oh!' But when Dubliners today are singing the hearty ballad, they might well be singing to the memory of a famous prostitute – the moll Malone!

The corner of Fishamble Street and Fishamble Street before re-development of Temple Bar. (Courtesy of GCI/harvest)

COPPERS AND ORANGES

Copper Alley was one of Dublin's most interesting medieval streets, linking Fishamble Street with Exchange Street (once called Blind Quay – a quay not on the river – and later Scarlet Lane) via Cow's Lane. It was famous for generations for its eating, coffee and gambling houses – and more besides! The Unicorn Tavern was one of its more famous taverns. Today, the once infamous Copper Alley runs through the reception area of Harding Hotel, parallel with Essex Street and Lord Edward Street. It dates from the thirteenth century and follows the route of an earlier Viking street. It was so narrow that carriages were unable to use it, though chairs or sedans could access it. In the fifteenth century the lane was known as Preston's Lane. By the early seventeenth century it became known as Copper Alley, taking its name from the copper money minted there. Lady Alice Fenton, who lived there during the 1600s, used to hand out copper money to the poor of the area. She used to clean the coins using oranges.

The area was notable for its publishers and printing presses. One notable publication was the 'Copper Alley Gazette' which appeared in 1766 in the *Freeman's Journal*. It contained a satirical account of the proceedings of politicians of the day. The *Freeman's Journal* was owned by the notorious 'Sham Squire' a highly controversial figure in his day. Real name Francis Higgins, he acquired the sobriquet early in life, after impersonating a gentleman of landed property and gaining the hand of a lady, who subsequently died of grief on discovering the reality. It was also he, it is alleged, who betrayed Lord Edward Fitzgerald during the 1798 Rebellion. Another notable publisher working on the street was Edward Waters, who printed one of Jonathan Swift's famous pamphlets denouncing England for interfering in Ireland's export trade of linen and woollens and rejecting anything wearable coming from England. The unfortunate Waters was arrested and tried but the jury found him not guilty, despite being sent back by the judge nine times to reconsider its verdict.[2]

Like the nearby Smock Alley, the area was full of brothels, the most famous one being the Maiden Tower. In fact Copper Alley was the very centre of a hectic and at times rowdy, public life.

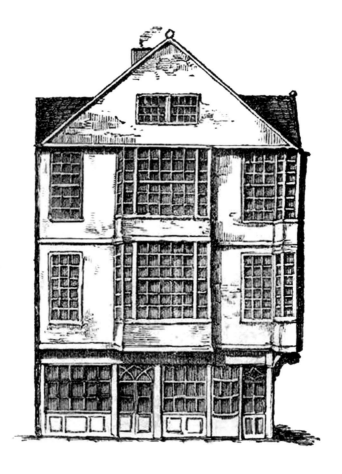

Dublin's last cagework house in Castle Street and typical of the kind of houses in the wider Hell area in the medieval period that survived until the seventeenth and eighteenth centuries. Published in the *Dublin Penny Journal*, 1813. (Courtesy of Comeheretome/archiseek)

DARKEY KELLY
AND PIMPING PEG

Late eighteenth-century Dublin was notorious for the conspic-
uous consumption and extravagant lifestyles of those of immense
wealth, power and prestige – all connected in some way or
another with Dublin Castle. The city was famed for its hedonistic
life. While those Irish living in a very cramped city mainly lived
a life of impoverishment, those with wealth and influence lived
extravagantly off the rents paid by their tenants outside the Pale.
It was a time of excessive wealth concentrated in the hands of the
ruling nobility and gentry, and thus a time of great licentious-
ness, debauchery, corruption and unbridled sexual activity with
the authorities turned a blind eye most of the time. It was also a
time of much building and re-development of Dublin combined
with the era being an age of extremes displaying stark contrasts
between those with or without.

As a result, Copper Alley, Smock Alley and the surrounding
lanes became home to an increasing number of brothels and
full of insalubrious characters, both male and female. As the
eighteenth century progressed, proximity to the Custom
House, the presence of the Irish Parliament, the large concentration of taverns, coffee houses, gambling houses, theatres and
high numbers of women living in poverty made the area from
Cork Hill to Blind Alley, from Copper Alley to Winetavern and

Cook Streets, and the surrounding streets and alleys, a centre of vice, gambling, drinking and prostitution.

Moreover, the location of Ireland's largest cockpit, the Cock Pit Royal, at Cork Hill, where the City Hall is now, was also a source of many customers for the local brothels. The Cock Pit Royal was a large area with tiered seating around it for customers, who placed bets on the outcome of the cockfighting. Sometimes up to twenty cocks fought at the same time, with gamblers placing bets on each of the cocks, but with only one winner. Cockfighting tournaments or festivals often lasted for at least a week and were a regular feature in the eighteenth century, when the sport was most popular. Cockfighting attracted gamblers from all parts of the country and there was also much drinking, carousing and, of course, visiting the local brothels.

The *Daily Gazetteer* for October 1736 reported the trial and conviction of a couple, the Reillys, for keeping a bawdy house. Both were sentenced to be whipped as bawdy house keepers. Mr Reilly was also given three months imprisonment, while his wife was paraded from Newgate Prison on Cornmarket to Trinity College, being whipped along the way. However, even as the debauchery increased the authorities remained generally lax in their attitudes towards prostitution (in fact it was never illegal) provided bawdy houses were not too disorderly. It was regarded as a necessary evil for men and a lewd or unfortunate activity for women.

Unsurprisingly, the prostitution trade reflected class divides of the day, not dissimilar from the present. Women from very poor and marginalised backgrounds engaged in street prosti-tution and were known as 'street-walkers', 'wantons', 'harlots', 'flaggers or flags' (because of the flag-stoned streets), 'fallen women', 'wretched', 'wicked', or 'loose' and sometimes 'molls'. They primarily dealt with men from the lower orders and charged a low price. Indoor brothels – 'bawdy houses' or 'houses of ill repute' – were controlled by madams and pimps, known as 'bawds', with the women known mainly as whores or molls, and were largely patronised by middle-class men; while 'courtesans' – often the illegitimate daughters of the upper classes – were organised by well-connected madams to meet the sexual needs of the wealthiest men (clients) in the highest echelons of Irish society. These latter women would not have been street-walkers and would not be seen in taverns or bawdy houses. They were often 'kept women' or 'mistresses', sticking with a wealthy client (known as a 'keeper') until one tired of the other or until his money ran out.

The courtesans would have been very much in touch with developments in the prostitution profession in London, since there was much travel between the two cities by the upper classes. In the mid-1700s a book was published, *Harris's Guide to Covent Garden Ladies*, that gave precise details as to the services provided, the prices charged, and a short physical description and temperament of the 'ladies of the night'.. One lady was described thus:

> … this accomplished nymph has just attained her eighteenth year, and fraught with every perfection, enters a volunteer in the field of Venus. She plays the pianoforte, sings, dances, and is the mistress of every manoeuvre in the amorous contest that can enhance the coming pleasure; is of middle stature, fine auburn hair, dark eyes and very inviting countenance, which ever seems to beam delight and love. In bed she is all the heart can wish, eyes admire, every limb is symmetry, ever action under cover truly amorous; her price two pounds.[1]

There were many houses of ill repute, disorderly houses and bawdy houses in the shadow of Christ Church Cathedral and in areas within walking distance of the cathedral, catering for all classes of customers – from the lowly and the poor who used the common streetwalker to the rich and famous such as the Governor of the Bank of Ireland or the Lord Lieutenant who liked illicit company but company appropriate to their social position – women such as Katherine Netterville (widely known as 'Kitty-Cut-a-Dash'), Laetitia Pilkington, Margaret Porter or Margaret Leeson. And these latter prostitutes picked their customers carefully, rather than the other way around. Prostitutes such as Mrs Anne Judge, Moll Hall and Mrs Dillon, brothel-keepers and procuresses, had no such standards, and were renowned for their promiscuity, wenches and bawdy houses. And there were other prostitutes such as Biddy Order and Mrs Brooks in Darby Square (off Werburgh Street) and brothels in Ross Lane, again near Werburgh Street, that catered specifically for the legal profession that had its base in the vicinity of the Christ Church Cathedral.[2]

The brothel business was the source of much violence, intimidation, kidnapping, rape and murder in Dublin. The owners used violence and bullying to retain their girls. In 1781 a prostitute was murdered in the Copper Alley area. In the same year, the brothel of Anne McDonagh, who had a stable of prostitutes in Little Booter Lane, was attacked by an angry mob after the murder of two more of her prostitutes. Mobs angrily attacking brothels was a feature of the closing decades of the eighteenth century, such was the brutal treatment meted out by brothel owners to prostitutes. McDonagh beat one of her girls so badly that she lost an eye. In 1791 four brothels had to be demolished by the authorities because of the level of violence.[3]

COPPER ALLEY AND THE MAIDEN TOWER

One of the most notorious brothels in Dublin in the eighteenth century was widely known as the Maiden Tower and was located in that most notorious of places – Copper Alley. This infamous establishment was where the most notorious of Hell prostitutes had her home and business. The lady in question was called Dorcas Kelly but was always referred as 'Darkey' Kelly because 'Dorcas' comes from the Irish word meaning 'dark' and also because of her flowing black hair and deep coal-black eyes set in a beautiful pale-skinned face. Her story was typical of the time – poverty and hardship forcing her into prostitution. Over time and using her sharp wits and wiles, she became a hard-headed business-woman and purchased the Maiden Tower, which she then had converted into a labyrinth of rooms, mirrors, false doors, secret passages, and a dungeon for the unwanted customers. This convoluted structure was said to be quite deliberate and it was quite impossible for any visitor to find his way out of the building unless accompanied by someone well acquainted with the intricacies of the building. Many unwary customers were lured to Darkey Kelly's brothel – and some were helped to disappear, their initial ecstasy quickly turning to pain. Murder was a frequent event in Hell and the Maiden Tower was not immune to such happenings, particularly if customers caused trouble or were murdered by enemies.[4]

Unfortunately for Darkey Kelly, she became embroiled in a murder case in which she was the defendant. The case involved her accusing Simon Luttrell, who in the 1760s was Sheriff of Dublin. This respectable position, however, had not prevented him from entertaining prostitutes and he had some involvement with Darkey Kelly's stable of prostitutes. She, being an opportunist, accused him of fathering her baby. Luttrell's family had owned Luttrellstown Castle, Castleknock, County Dublin since the early thirteenth century. He was made Baron Irnham of Luttrellstown in 1768 and became First Earl of Carhampton in 1785. In his younger days he was one of the most active members of the notorious Hellfire Club, which held meetings in nearby Eagle Tavern on Cork Hill. His rakish behaviour earned him the nickname 'King of Hell' and he was reputed to have helped the English upper-class socialite and courtesan Mary Nesbitt in her career by seducing her. Nesbitt was born Mary Davis, in poverty and of unknown parentage. Her later enemies accused her of being 'born in a wheelbarrow' in Covent Garden. Her career began as an artist's model for the famous painter Joshua Reynolds, and through this connection she began her career as a courtesan. Thanks to her meeting Simon Luttrell, she was subsequently known as 'Hellfire Davis'. And thanks to him she was introduced to Alexander Nesbitt of the London merchant banking family, whom she later married.

In an age of extremes, Darkey Kelly's opportunism was understandable but unfortunately for her failed. After accusing Luttrell of being the father of her supposed baby in the hope of financial gain, he refused to acknowledge her accusation and instead claimed she was a witch and had actually murdered her child. These rumours of witchcraft were deliberately spread around Dublin, and she found herself in deep trouble. Some said that her having customers from the ascendancy was her downfall. It was said that men such as Simon Luttrell 'wanted the wench, but not the woman', whereas she 'wanted the name but not the man'. Despite being accused of witchcraft, the real

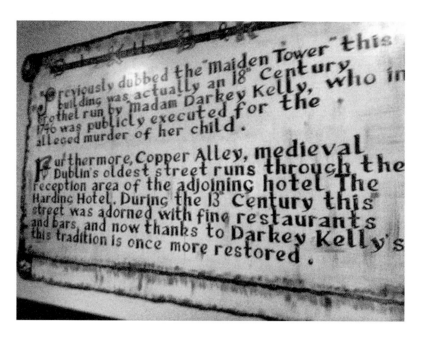

Plaque on wall of Harding's Hotel, Fishamble Street. (Courtesy of Harding's Hotel/Lisa J)

charge against her was much more serious. Contemporary newspaper reports showed that on examination of the Maiden Tower, investigators found five bodies in the dungeon, customers who had been murdered for various reasons. Consequently she was tried for the murder of John Dowling, a local shoemaker. She was sentenced to death in January 1764, and was publicly burned at Stephen's Green shortly afterwards. Women in eighteenth-century Ireland were second-class citizens and the manner in which executions were carried out reflected that blatant divide – men found guilty of murder were merely hanged, whereas women were throttled first, and then burnt. After Darkey Kelly's execution, prostitutes rioted in Copper Alley.[6]

The Darkey Kelly case did not end there. Her sister was involved in another sensational news story in the 1780s when Simon Luttrell's son Henry, who also had the title Lord Carhampton, and who was involved in the revived Hellfire Club, allegedly raped a young teenage girl in a brothel. The girl was procured for him by brothel-keeper Maria Llewellyn. Following the accusations, Henry Luttrell reportedly had the young girl and her parents falsely imprisoned. The girl's mother died in prison and Luttrell's trumped up charges against the girl and her family were later dismissed in court. Llewellyn was described as Darkey Kelly's sister, and she was condemned to be hanged in 1788. However, on the morning she was to be hanged, the Lord Lieutenant pardoned her as there were doubts over the testimony of witnesses. However, one of Llewellyn's pimps, Robert Edgeworth (known as Squire Edgeworth), was sentenced and jailed for perjury. As part of his punishment he endured a spell in the stocks outside the Tholsel at Skinners Row (Christ Church Place). The crowd pelted him with rotten eggs and snow balls. In 1789 he went into the stocks again. This time he received rotten eggs, oranges, potatoes, old shoes, brickbats, dead cats, mud and filth of every kind. Today, the stocks may be seen across the road in the crypt of the cathedral.

Such stories frequently occurred in the tawdry and dangerous world of prostitution in Dublin in the eighteenth century. Mary Davis was lucky in her dealings with Luttrell – unfortunately Darkey Kelly was not.[5]

PIMPING PEG:
QUEEN OF THE BROTHELS

The story of the top end of the prostitution profession in eighteenth-century Dublin is captured in the life and times of the beautiful adventurous Margaret Leeson. She is sometimes regarded as Ireland's first brothel-owning 'madam', and she was a fascinating woman. She would become the most famous, the wealthiest, and the most fashionable of Ireland's eighteenth-century madams and even published her memoirs in 1797, opening the work by noting 'I shall now commence with the most memorable epoch of my unfortunate life ...' Because of her prowess and networking skills in the late eighteenth-century Dublin Georgian social scene, as well as her intelligence, charm and beauty, she was able to recruit many from the top echelons of that society as her clients For many years she was the talk of the town, what with her jewellery, her dresses, her carriages, her clients and her girls.

The secret and often tragic life of Margaret Leeson, also known as Peg Plunkett and Pimping Peg, started in 1727 when she was born in Killough, County Westmeath, the daughter of a wealthy Catholic landowner who was related to the Earl of Cavan. But her idyllic rural childhood was shattered when her mother and eldest brother died and Margaret's father passed control of his estates to his cruel son Christopher, who badly treated his young sister. She eventually escaped to Dublin. Here she met a man called Dardis who introduced her to a life of prostitution.

From the age of 15 – after she became pregnant and was abandoned by her upper-class seducer – Margaret Leeson effectively navigated upper-class society to ensure her survival, first as the 'kept woman' of a succession of wealthy men and later as the operator of a lucrative, high-end brothel frequented by the rich and famous of the day. She met a Mr Leeson, a wealthy English merchant from whom she took her assumed name so as to enhance her respectability. Mr Leeson fell for Margaret's charms and put her up in a house in Ranelagh. But while Leeson was away she would sneak in to the house of her other lover, a John Lawless (Buck Lawless). On discovering her infidelity, Leeson abandoned her and left her penniless. She was later to write of him in her memoirs that she was more 'distressed by the loss of his purse that the loss of his person'.[7] Lawless went on to become her longest partner. They lived together for five years and had five children. But, as ever, tragedy struck. Their money eventually ran out, the children died one by one and Lawless left for America, leaving Margaret heartbroken.

She returned to a life of prostitution and found that many wealthy men were willing to entertain her and pay her way. She soon regained her position in high society, and her first brothel in Dublin was opened on Drogheda Street (now O'Connell Street). However, this brothel was closed owing to the vandalism of a group called the 'Pinking Dindies', led by Richard Crosbie (1755–1800), duellist and aeronaut (he famously landed a balloon in Ranelagh Gardens). Not to be deterred, on receiving compensation from Crosbie she set up a new brothel with her right-hand woman and fellow courtesan Sally Hayes. Her latest venture was a luxurious brothel, fitted out with every comfort and boasting prostitutes hand-picked by Margaret herself. It became a well-known establishment amongst well-bred men, and her clients included a Lord Lieutenant, Charles Manners, Fourth Duke of Rutland, who insisted on sleeping only with Margaret, swearing he would pay his fortune if only his wife was as good in bed as she was. It was because of her relationship with the Duke that she received approval in Dublin's social circles. She refused, however, to have as a client another Lord Lieutenant, John Fane, the Earl of Westmoreland, because of his ill-treatment of his wife. The famous Huguenot banker David La Touche, whose name still lives on in Dublin financial circles, was the Governor of the Bank of Ireland and one of the most distinguished visitors to her brothels. Other important clients included Walter Butler, Viscount Thurles, later the Earl of Ormond; Captain Francis Craddock, aide-de-camp in 1783 to the Lord Lieutenant; Richard Daly of the Theatre Royal and Smock Alley Theatre; and Joseph Leeson, first Earl of Milltown, known as 'Game Cock Joe'. However, she also listed among her clients, earls, generals, top barristers, merchants, aldermen, writers, clergymen and many others at the top levels of every influential area of society. Most of these men had their own 'kept woman' or mistress. Society functions were always attended by many of Dublin's top-class prostitutes, and some of those came from the environs of the Smock Alley Theatre and Hell; they blended in and were readily welcomed.[8]

Mrs Leeson had a wicked sense of humour and on one occasion attended one of Dublin's famous Masquerade Balls dressed as Diana, Goddess of Virginity! She had her girls dressed in similar mocking attire. On another occasion when the celebrated violinist Signor Carnavalli was involved in playing at Italian operas in the Smock Alley Theatre, Mrs Leeson was refused entry because of her reputation. Seemingly, the violinist had certain standards and did not wish to have in the theatre ladies of her description. However, such was her indignation and outrage at this that she immediately got a court warrant and returned to the theatre and had Carnavalli and the ushers consigned to nearby Newgate Jail. Paradoxically, she had no difficulty in casting aspersions on others, as is shown when she challenged the English Prince Regent in the course of some of her frequent visits to London. Once, when she was browsing in the same outfitters as the prince, she deliberately bought the same waistcoat, loudly proclaiming that her purchase was for her shoemaker. Another time, she and the prince crossed swords on a road when she refused to make way for his entourage. Instead, she rode alongside his carriage shouting in that they were both equally entitled to use the road and that the Irish had no intention of adhering to English practices of servility.[9]

That she was particularly courageous or brazen is obvious from the events of another of her regular visits to the Smock Alley Theatre, this time with a coterie of her girls. One of her regular clients, Charles Manners, the Duke of Rutland, was also in attendance, sitting in the regal box. Of course, some of the less prosperous theatregoers sitting in the cheaper gallery seats noticed and one hollered up provocatively, asking Mrs Leeson, whom they knew as 'Peg', as to who had slept with her the previous night. Not to be outdone, Mrs Leeson, in a bold voice and slyly glancing at the Regal Box, heartily riposted, 'manners, you dogs!'[10]

In the late 1700s, and after thirty years in the business, she decided to reform and cash in all the promissory notes she had accumulated. However, she became penniless in the process, as former clients refused to pay or had disappeared. Consequently, she ended up in a debtor's prison. By this time she was not only penniless but she had lost her once strikingly beautiful looks. However, a few of her former admirers did help her. Francis Higgins, the Sham Squire and owner of the *Freeman's Journal*, provided some assistance. Bishop Harvey of Derry, who was also the Earl of Bristol and her former client, sent her some money. Despite this, she attempted suicide. Later she was forced to write her memoirs in a bid to raise some cash. Published in 1794, two volumes appeared, to the embarrassment of many. The full title of her work is: *The Life of Mrs. Margaret Leeson alias Peg Plunket: Written by herself; in which are given anecdotes, sketches of the lives and bon mots of some of the most celebrated characters in Great-Britain and Ireland, particularly of all the filles des joys and men of pleasure and gallantry, which have usually frequented her Citherean temple for these thirty years past.*

Inside front
cover of
Margaret
Leeson's book
recounting her
memoirs as
Pimping Peg,
courtesan and
brothel-keeper.

MEMOIRS

OF

MRS. MARGARET LEESON,

WRITTEN BY HERSELF;

IN WHICH ARE GIVEN ANECDOTES SKETCHES OF THE
LIVES AND BON MOTS OF SOME OF THE
MOST CELEBRATED

CHARACTERS

IN

GREAT-BRITAIN AND IRELAND,

PARTICULARLY OF ALL THE

FILLES DES JOYS

AND

MEN OF PLEASURE AND GALLANTRY

WHICH HAVE USUALLY FREQUENTED HER CITHEREAN
TEMPLE FOR THESE THIRTY YEARS PAST.

In Leeson's memoirs she also complains that Dublin was home to many men who 'however they might be deemed gentlemen at their birth, or connections, yet, by their actions, deserved no other appellation than that of RUFFIANS.' The third volume and the first to name names was in manuscript when she was attacked and raped.[11] As in the fate of Darkey Kelly, the brutal realities of the sex trade in eighteenth-century Dublin are captured in the final chapter of the life of Margaret Lesson. She died from the rape and the resulting complications of venereal disease, at the age of 70, broken and alone. It has been said that had there been a guard of honour at her funeral it would have stretched from Parliament House to Dublin Castle.

One of her professional friends, Mary (Moll) Hall, who had a similar sad and lonely demise, had for years run a brothel in Mecklenburgh Street, in a house bought for her by an admirer. Mecklenburgh Street, just off Lower Gardiner Street, was a street lined with fine and expensive Georgian houses, attracting only the very wealthy purchasers. Margaret Leeson had visited and stayed in this house on many occasions. Moll Hall was not the only high-class prostitute to set up business in Mecklenburgh Street in the late 1700s. Mary Fagan, also known as Mary Crosbie, another friend of Margaret's, had a similar enterprise on the same street, this time bought by her 'keeper', a Captain Misset. These madams only attracted the very best clients, with vast financial resources. It was these madams who began the tradition of brothels in this part of Dublin. So it may be argued that there was a direct link between the brothels of mid- and late eighteenth-century Dublin located in and around Hell and the subsequent rise of an equally notorious area called Monto – Moll Hall might well have been the first madam of Monto.[12]

THE EAGLE TAVERN, THE BLASTERS AND THE HELLFIRE CLUB

As is evident in the life and times of Pimping Peg, debauchery and immorality were to be found on a grand scale in the eighteenth century among the upper classes in Dublin. However, there was also carousing of a more sinister nature. A House of Lords' Committee Report of 1737 found that there existed in Dublin a club called the 'Blasters' or 'The Hellfire Club '.

Clubs were an essential aspect of the eighteenth-century urban male lifestyle. They provided a location for the 'young bucks' to carouse in. They were exclusive, mainly populated by a class of rich and landed gentry. In 1719–20, the first of the Hellfire Clubs in England was started by Sir Francis Dashwood in Buckinghamshire, and quickly became notorious for rumours about sexual orgies and tales of the occult. The Hellfire Clubs of Ireland seemingly took their inspiration from him and involved themselves in idleness, luxury, profanity, gambling and drinking. They went in for outrageous activities such as daring blasphemies including playing cards on Sunday, reading Lucretius and eating pigeon ('Holy Ghost') pie. Blasphemy and black magic were an intrinsic part of the Hellfire legend. Their members were mostly young, male and moneyed, united by an enduring fascination with the forbidden fruit offered by the Devil, and a continuing flirtation with danger and the unknown. Temptation led naturally to rampant hedonism; no appetite went unsated. Thumbing their noses (or worse) at Church, State and civil society, they drank to excess, leered at pornography and goaded each other on. They were elitist clubs in which hedonism ruled in a mix of sociability and rampant sexuality that led to excess, says Evelyn Lord in her book, *The Hell-Fire Clubs: Sex, Satanism and Secret Societies.*[1]

Dublin at this time was expanding and there was an increasing prosperity in certain areas and among certain classes – notably the ascendancy. The young Anglo-Irish aristocracy caroused around the fashionable and not so fashionable parts of Dublin, including Hell. Walking sticks were part of their attire as they swaggered around the fine Georgian squares and streets and one Dublin shop even sold such sticks with the words 'who dare sneeze' and 'who is afraid?' emblazoned on them. Most of them found their common ground in ceremonial drinking and dining or in gambling venues, but a few allegedly focused on sex, blasphemy and deliberate ill-doing and formed what became known as the Dublin Hellfire Club,[2] which meat in the Eagle Tavern, in Hell.

Dublin's Hellfire Club was consequently one of several exclusive establishments using the name Hellfire Club that existed in Britain and Ireland in the eighteenth century. However, the outrageous alleged activities of the Dublin Hellfire Club – provocative blasphemy, taboo sexual activities, atrocities and the habit of toasting the devil – have become the stuff of legend.

THE KING OF HELL

The Eagle Tavern was situated on Cork Hill. Cork Hill derived its name from Richard Boyle, First Earl of Cork in the mid-1600s. It has a chequered history, both socially and architecturally. It was originally lined with the mansions of the well-heeled of Dublin society but many of the buildings were subsequently demolished to make way for the Royal Exchange, the development of Parliament Street and the opening of Lord Edward Street.

But before that demolition took place, Cork Hill, beside Copper Alley and stretching to Wood and Essex Quay, Smock and Blind Alley, was, like all the surrounding area, a veritable rabbit warren of alleys, lanes and winding passages that might lead to anywhere. It was on the edge of Hell and like this notorious district it was very dangerous for the unwary. There was no public lighting at night and it had no night watch.

The Dublin Hellfire Club was founded in around 1735 by some of the elite of the Protestant ascendancy, including Richard Parsons, First Earl of Rosse and the humorous artist James Worsdale. The club motto was *'Fais ce que tu voudras'* – 'Do as thou wilt' – and its mascot was a black cat. Besides the Eagle Tavern itself, the many taverns, coffee houses, brothels and gambling houses in the area of Cork Hill, Copper Alley, Smock

Members of the Hellfire Club in the eighteenth century. (Courtesy of Come Here to Me/Donal Fallon)

Alley, Fishamble Street and Winetavern Street were their haunts. Taverns, eating houses and coffee houses were social centres for meetings, political groups, concerts and billiards. During the first half of the eighteenth century the two most fashionable meeting places were both on Cork Hill – the Eagle Tavern and Lucas's Coffee House, immediately opposite. The notorious Colonel Henry Luttrell was murdered in 1717 while going home one night in a hackney chair from Lucas's Coffee House. Daly's Coffee House on College Green was the most notorious gambling den and Dick's Coffee House on nearby Skinners Row was equally famous in the city, but attracted a more educated and culturally refined clientele. The Eagle Tavern was also the venue for clubs like the Aughrim Club, the Sportsman's Club and the Hanover Club. In 1739 a dinner for members of the Hanover Club consisted of more than 200 dishes.

In 1755 the Duke of Hamilton and his Irish bride, Elizabeth Gunning, who was a celebrated beauty at the time in Ireland and England, visited the Eagle Tavern, and huge crowds witnessed the occasion. Other taverns crammed into this area included the Hoop Tavern, the Cock and Punch Bowl. However, the Eagle Tavern and Lucas's stood out, for they were the most dangerous, with the yard behind being the scene of numerous duels and brawls. Customers gambled on the possible outcome of the duels. It was often referred to as 'the surgeon's hall', such was the frequency of bodies, either dead or requiring urgent medical care, there.[3]

One of the club's most notorious characters was Richard Parsons, who was equally famous for his profligacy and his wit. He was given the title 'King of Hell' in recognition of the club's location and name (it was also known as 'the Devil's Kitchen). Given his personality, it is not surprising that he was particularly fond of the company of prostitutes, and there were plenty in the locality of Hell. But he did not limit himself to Hell's prostitutes; he at times preferred the company higher-society prostitutes, 'kept women' or madams, such as Mrs Laetitia Pilkington. He was said to have often dressed like Satan and had his own special chair to oversee proceedings in the Eagle Tavern.

The first toast at the Hellfire Club was always drunk to the absent devil and it was said that they left a chair vacant at each gathering, in case the Devil chose to make an appearance. A satirical ballad was also recited in which the Devil was represented as summoning before him those who had the strongest claims to succeed him as King of Hell. Simon Luttrell (later Baron Irnham), a member of the Hellfire Club was introduced in the ballad, which concluded:

> But as he spoke there issued from the crowd
> Irnham the base, the cruel, and the proud
> And eager cried, 'I boast superior claim
> To Hell's dark throne, and Irnham is my name'.[4]

Accounts of the club's meetings claim that members drank 'scaltheen', a mixture of whiskey, eggs and hot butter. It was as strong as poteen and had similar hallucinatory effects on the drinker's well-being or otherwise. The club was also infamous for excessive whiskey drinking and general debauchery. In the 1740s, whiskey became very popular when the excise duty was lowered and it became much cheaper.

Lord Rosse was probably the president of the Eagle Tavern-based Hellfire Club. He gladly embraced 'all the vices which the beau monde calls pleasure', according to Peter Somerville Large in his book on Dublin. Another member, Lord Santry, was found guilty by the House of Lords of having killed a man in a drunken fray. In 1739, at the age of 29, he stabbed to death a servant named Laughlin Murphy with his sword for the spurious reason of speaking out of turn. This was a major scandal at the time but he was subsequently pardoned (as was the case in general when the ascendancy misbehaved). Evidence of the identities of other members of the club comes from a painting by Worsdale (one of the founders) entitled *The Hellfire Club, Dublin*, now held by the National Gallery of Ireland, which shows five members of the club seated around a table. The five men are Henry, Fourth Baron of Santry; Simon Luttrell, Lord Irnham; Colonel Henry Ponsonby; Colonel Richard St George and Colonel Clements. Years later, during excavations in the vicinity of the former Eagle Tavern, the skeleton of a dwarf, reputed to have been sacrificed by members of the Hellfire Club, was found.[5]

THE MOUNTPELIER HILL CONNECTION

Mountpelier Hill is located in Rathfarnham, County Dublin and is a small hill about 400m (1,200ft) in height. The ruined building at the summit is popularly referred to as the Hellfire Club, its popular name. According to the architectural historian, Maurice Craig, it is possible that the Hellfire Club, based at Cork Hill, may at times have exchanged the confines of the city taverns for the more bracing hilltop hunting lodge. This building – built around 1725 by William Conolly, Speaker of the Irish House of Commons – was originally called Mountpelier and since its construction the hill has also gone by the same name. But over the years the lodge has also been known as 'The Haunted House', 'The Shooting Lodge', 'The Kennel', and 'Conolly's Folly'. Coincidentally, William Conolly had purchased Mountpelier from Philip, Duke of Wharton, founder of the first Hellfire Club in 1719.

The identity of the architect is unknown. Rathfarnham author Michael Fewer has suggested it may have been Edward Lovett Pearce (1699–1733) who was employed by Conolly to carry out works at Castletown House in 1724. While the building has a rough appearance today, the architecture is of Palladian design. The upper floor consisted of a hall and two reception rooms. On the eastern side, there was a third, timber-floored level where the sleeping quarters were located. On the ground floor was a kitchen, servants' quarters and stairs to the upper floors. The entrance, which is on the upper floor, was reached by a long flight of stairs which is now missing. At each side of the building was a room with a lean-to roof which may have been used to stable horses. A stone mounting block to assist people onto their horses can be seen on the eastern side. To the front there was a semi-circular courtyard, enclosed by a low stone wall and entered by a gate. The house faces to the north, looking over Dublin and the plains of Meath and Kildare, including Conolly's primary residence at Castletown House in Celbridge.

The grounds around the lodge consisted of a 1,000-acre deer park. Originally there was a cairn with a prehistoric passage grave on the summit. Stones from the cairn were taken and used in the construction of the lodge. A nearby standing stone was also used for the lintel over the fireplace. Shortly after completion, a storm blew the roof off. Conolly had the roof replaced with an arched stone roof constructed in a similar fashion to that of a bridge. This roof has remained intact to the present day, even though the building has been abandoned for over two centuries and despite the roof being set alight with tar barrels during the visit of Queen Victoria to Ireland in 1849.[6] Local superstition attributed this incident to the work of the Devil, a punishment for interfering with the cairn. Since this time, Mountpelier Hill has become associated with numerous paranormal events. There is little evidence that the lodge was put to much use. Conolly himself died in 1729. However, it was the period in the years following Conolly's death that Mountpelier's association with the Hellfire Club of the Eagle Tavern on Cork Hill began.

The already suspect reputation was further enhanced by rumours that members of the Hellfire Club were using Mountpelier Lodge as a meeting place after it was let to the club by the Conolly family. Numerous lurid stories of wild behaviour and debauchery as well as occult practices and demonic manifestations have become part of the local folklore. However, it is not clear to what extent the Hellfire Club made use of the building. There are almost no verifiable accounts of the activities that went on there, although Michael Fewer has suggested that this is due to the remoteness of its location rather than a lack of activity.

Nonetheless, numerous (very doubtful) stories surrounding the building have become part of local folklore. One of the best known of these tells of a stranger who arrived at the club on a stormy night. Invited in, he joined the members in a card game. One player dropped his card on the floor and when he bent under the table to retrieve it noticed that the stranger had cloven hooves. At this point the visitor disappeared in a ball of flame. Another story tells of a priest who came to the house one night and found the members engaged in the sacrifice of a black leopard. The priest grabbed the leopard and uttered an exorcism, upon which a demon was released from the corpse of the leopard.

Another story centres on club member Simon Luttrell. Luttrell is believed to have been the subject of *The Diaboliad*, a 1777 poem dedicated to 'the worst man in England'. According to the story, Luttrell made a pact with the Devil to give up his soul within seven years in return for settling his debts, but when the Devil came to the Mountpelier lodge to claim his prize Luttrell distracted him and fled. Other tales recount numerous drinking sessions and black masses at which animal sacrifices, and on one occasion the sacrifice of a dwarf, took place.

At some point during this period, the building was damaged by fire. There are several stories connected with this incident. One holds that the club set fire to the building when William Conolly's son refused to renew the lease on the lodge. An alternative story claims the club members started the fire to give the building a hellish appearance. Another story recounts that, following a black mass, a footman spilled a drink on Richard Chapell 'Burn-Chapel' Whaley's coat. Whaley retaliated by pouring brandy over the man and setting him alight. The fire spread around the building and killed many members. Following the fire, the club relocated further down the hill to Killakee Stewards House. However, the club's activities declined after this incident. Whaley was a hugely controversial figure, particularly renowned for burning Catholic churches, and hence his name.[7]

BUCK WHALEY AND THE
REVIVAL OF THE HELLFIRE CLUB

The Hellfire Club was disbanded in 1741 after its main founder, Lord Rosse, died – but not before having one last laugh. When he lay on his deathbed, the rector of St Anne's church on Dawson Street, around the corner from his house on Molesworth Street, wrote to him imploring him to repent his evil ways while there was still time. Lord Rosse was amused by the letter and noticing that it was addressed to him as just 'My Lord', but with no name, he re-sealed the letter and sent it to Lord Kildare, who was well known for his upstanding life and piety. When Kildare received it he was initially furious with the rector, until the truth came out.

Between his death in 1741 and the revival of the club in the 1770s, a number of other similar clubs developed in Dublin. These include the Holy Fathers and the Cherokee Club (based on the name of an American Indian tribe), dedicated to their own pleasure and amusement, scant respect for women, violence and duelling, copious drinking, disorderly outrages, blasphemy, general nuisance and mayhem, extravagant and startlingly colourful uniforms – all based on the excessive behaviour of the Hellfire Club and a made up of young members of the upper classes in Irish society.[8]

The Hellfire Club was revived in 1771 and was active for a further thirty years. Its most notorious member was Thomas 'Buck' Whaley, born in 1755 and son 'Burn-Chapel' Whaley. He was elected to the Irish House of Commons in 1785. On his father's death he inherited a fortune and devoted his time to squandering his new wealth in drinking, gambling and carousing. He fitted rather well into the revived Hellfire Club. Meetings once again took place at Mountpelier Lodge and, according to one story, the members kidnapped, murdered and ate a farmer's daughter. Whaley won great fortunes at the gaming tables as well as partaking in some bizarre wagers. In one wager he won £25,000 from the Duke of Leinster by riding to Jerusalem and back within a year. This was not a religious pilgrimage and he later boasted of playing handball against the Walls of Jerusalem and having drunk his way there. On another occasion, for a bet of £12,000, he rode a beautiful white Arab stallion in a death-defying leap from the drawing room on the second floor of his father's house on Stephen's Green, over a carriage parked outside the door and onto the street over 30ft below. He won his wager, surviving with a broken leg, but the horse was killed in the jump.

Less tumultuous times in the 1940s. Cycling past the area formerly called Hell. (Courtesy of Fotofinish)

Remorse, however, overcame Buck Whaley with the passage of time and so he resolved to seek absolution for his sins. Whilst praying in St Audoen's church, which overlooked Hell, he had a vision of the Devil creeping down the aisle towards him. Seized with terror, he ran from the church and fled Ireland forever. Whaley eventually repented and when he died in 1800 the Irish Hellfire Club passed away with him forever.

The antiquarian Austin Cooper visited Mountpelier in 1779 and found it in a state of disrepair. Joseph Holt, a general in the Society of the United Irishmen, recorded in his memoirs that he spent a night in the ruins while on the run following the 1798 Rebellion. The Conollys sold the lands to Luke White in 1800. These passed, by way of inheritance to the Massey family of Duntrileage, County Limerick. When the Massy family became bankrupt, the lands were acquired by the State. Today, the building is maintained by Coillte, who manage the forestry plantations on Mountpelier's slopes and who have installed concrete stairs and iron safety rails across the upper windows. It is well worth a visit and has an unrivalled view of Dublin City.[9]

THE BLACK DOG, THE BLACK PIG AND HELL

The name of the area called Hell survived well into the nineteenth century, as a story about the Black Dog in the *Dublin Penny Journal* confirms. The Black Dog was a name given to Newgate Prison because of a nearby tavern of the same name.

There is a legend associated with the prison about a mysterious inmate known as Olocher. The old *Dublin Penny Journal* of 1832 (a weekly newspaper that included James Clarence Mangan, born at no. 3 Fishamble Street, among its writers) recorded that Olocher had been sentenced to death for rape and murder. However, he was found to have committed suicide on the morning of his execution. Shortly afterwards several women were reportedly attacked by a demonic black pig, which they christened the Dolocher, assuming it was the incarnation of Olocher.

When one of the jail's sentries went missing and the attacks intensified, a band of men set out one night from a public house in nearby Cook Street, determined to slaughter every black pig they encountered. When morning came, not a pig, white or black, could be seen. However, according to the *Dublin Penny Journal*, 'Next winter the Dolocher re-appeared! A young woman passing by Fisher's Alley on the Wood Quay, was pulled in and a bundle of clothes which she had in her hand, beside her cloak, dragged from her. The alarm spread again; the Dolocher recommenced his 'reign of terror'; women fled the streets, especially about Fisher's Alley and Christ Church Lane, and even the stouter hearts of men trembled at thought of encountering so dire a combatant. Yet strange, very strange to say, the demon beast confined his assaults to the fairer sex.[1]

Months later a drunken blacksmith borrowed a cloak from a female acquaintance and set out for home. The story goes, that 'just as the blacksmith reached Hell, out rushed the Dolocher, pounced on its victim, and pinned him against the wall. The blacksmith was not a man to die easy at any time, and especially with a drop of the rale stuff in his noddle. He raised his muscular arm: 'Be ye Dolocher or Devil, or what ye may, take that!' he yelled, letting fall a thumper that would have staggered Dan Donnelly.'

A crowd gathered and the demon was revealed to be the missing sentry: 'A crowd cautiously collected; the dying and groaning devil was lifted up, and out of a black pig's skin came

Hard times as shown by Dublin's Rag Market in the shadow of St Patrick's Cathedral, 1903. (Courtesy of Dublin Forums/jembo)

the very man who had been carried off, body and soul, from his post at the BLACK DOG.' Before he died he confessed to aiding Olocher in his suicide and orchestrating the slaughter of the pigs for the purpose of attacking and robbing innocent citizens. And as fast as the pigs were killed they 'were removed to a cellar in Schoolhouse-lane, and that thus he had kept up the delusion for the purpose of robbery'.[2]

SNUFF BOXES AND THE END OF HELL

Eventually Hell ceased to be a den of iniquity and debauchery because of street widening and redevelopment in the area, particularly the building and widening of the streets of Christ Church Place, Cork Hill and Lord Edward Street. When Fishamble Street, Winetavern Street and the adjacent area were improved, re-configured and widened, the lane called Hell finally disappeared. This was also facilitated by the nineteenth-century refurbishment of Christ Church Cathedral, which included the erection of railings around the perimeter of the church, separating it from the former Skinners Row (now Christ Church Place and much widened). The railings effectively closed off the lane called Hell, although two gates erected in vicinity of the entrances to Hell from St Michael's Hill and Fishamble Street are still there today.

The wooden image of Satan that had been above the gateway leading into Hell was carved into much sought-after carved oblong snuff boxes, which became collectors' most valued items. Some of these included a depiction of the Devil escorting a figure to the fires of Hell. And on the inside of the snuff box lid the following lines were engraved:

Prime your nose well,
I'd have you be civil,

This box was in Hell,
And was made of the Devil.[1]

On the completion of the new Four Courts on Inn's Quay, across the River Liffey, in 1796, the courts in the grounds of Christ Church Cathedral were finally no more; the Tholsel on Skinners Row became City Hall at the junction of Parliament Street, Dame Street and Cork Hill. The buildings in the grounds to the front of Christ Church Cathedral were demolished. Christ Church Lane became St Michael's Hill. The arch linking the cathedral to the new Synod Hall was built over the hill.

Christ Church Yard likewise disappeared in the nineteenth century. The present site of the Royal Exchange (now Rates Office) opposite City Hall, formerly occupied by a range of old houses, taverns and coffee houses along Cork Hill, which were all demolished, was built on a huge rock which extends along Parliament Street, under Capel Street Bridge and to the north side of the River Liffey. It was well-known as Stand Fast Dick. The Royal Exchange retains one of the finest late eighteenth-century interiors in Dublin. All these changes combined to spell out the end to the 'good' times in the area called Hell.

With these changes the more common brothels and prostitutes moved to the nearby Liberties areas of The Coombe, Meath and Francis Streets. Here, the name of Hell was not forgotten and was used for a time to describe the area around the junction of The Coombe and the lower ends of these streets. There were lodging houses, tenement houses and second-hand clothes shops in abundance in this old area of Dublin. The oldest profession in the world continued here under the guise of some of the second-hand clothes shops. According to Revd Whitelaw in 1805, who was based in St Catherine's church, Thomas Street, and looked at the slum problem in his parish, '[of the] street walkers that infest the more opulent parts of the city, a large proportion issues from the Liberty'.

One hundred years later, the situation had barely changed. In the early twentieth century, Jesuit priest Fr John Gwynn bemoaned the fact that Sackville Street (O'Connell Street) was the stomping ground of prostitutes seeking business: 'from the Coombe and other parts of the city … crowds of young girls take possession of the city when the darkness comes, and whose demeanour by no means suggests the modesty and decorum we are wont to regard as inseparable from the Irish maiden.'[2]

Interestingly, and not too far from this latter area, the junction of Patrick Street, New Street, Dean Street and Kevin Street was known for years as the 'Four Corners of Hell'. The name here however, derived not from prostitution, but from the fact of having four pubs – one on each corner. The title arose when a Mission priest, who was trying to persuade the local people to desist from drinking alcohol in these establishments because of the enormous social consequences for families of the addicted, very vociferously said in the course of his sermon, that the pubs were nothing less than the 'four corners of Hell'!

St Michael's Hill,
c. 1900.
(Courtesy of GCI)

WHISKEY TO THE RESCUE: THE DISTILLER'S CHURCH

As we have seen, Christ Church Cathedral witnessed many changes over the years, but by the 1800s it had fallen into disrepair. As in the case of St Patrick's Cathedral (called 'The Brewer's Church' after help to restore it came from the Guinness family), a wealthy Dublin man came to the rescue and donated £230,000 to restore it.

It is quite ironic that some of the notoriety surrounding the crypt of the cathedral and Hell derived from the sale of alcohol and it was the alcohol industry that came to the rescue of the cathedral in the late 1800s. The name of this man was Henry Roe and he made his money by distilling whiskey in nearby Thomas Street. During this heyday of Geo. Roe & Co., Thomas Street, Henry Roe applied a substantial portion of the Roe distillery wealth to the restoration of Christ Church Cathedral and the building of the attached Synod Hall (today housing the tourist attraction, Dublinia). Between 1871 and 1878, he donated the astronomical sum of £220,000 to £250,000. Henry Roe turned the cathedral into the building Dubliners know today, but while the outside was substantially changed the inside stayed much as it had been since the Middle Ages, including the crypt. Following its restoration, a new thoroughfare was cut in the vicinity of Christ Church, and although it was named 'Lord Edward Street', a local witticism at the time was 'Roe Row',[3] and the cathedral was often called 'The Distiller's Church'.

Today, the crypt of the cathedral contains various monuments and historical features, including the oldest known secular carvings in Ireland: two carved statues that until the late eighteenth century stood outside the Tholsel (Dublin's medieval city hall, which was demolished in 1806). The crypt also contains other historical artefacts which have survived here simply because they were in no one's way. The stocks, formerly in Christ Church Place, made in 1670 and used for the punishment of offenders before the Court of the Dean's Liberty (the small area under the cathedral's exclusive civic authority), are to be found here. Offenders

Winetavern Street from St Michael's Hill. (Courtesy of GCI)

were locked in the stocks for the prescribed period while 'friends' often pelted them with rotten fruit or vegetables. Another item of interest is the cat and the rat, the one presumably chasing the other, which were trapped in an organ pipe in the 1860s and became mummified. According to a local wit, 'Egypt might have Tutankhamun but Ireland has Tom and Gerry!'[4]

A visitor to the crypt may still see the original part of it, where the tavern was located, that was called 'Hell'. It is still called by that name by the staff of the cathedral but is now used for storage purposes. There is a passage leading directly from John's Lane East via a back door of the cathedral straight along another passage to the door of this former tavern. The cobblestoned passage outside the John's Lane East entrance is marked by a dagger and wattle symbol of a former Viking house that stood in the area. If one enters through this door, Hell is in front of you!

BENBURB STREET, PORTOBELLO AND THE CURRAGH WRENS

Despite the demise of Hell, the oldest profession in the world did not cease business. Instead it moved elsewhere – to parts of the Liberties and other areas of the city. In the early nineteenth century, the Dublin Metropolitan Police (DMP) statistics show that 2,849 arrests for prostitution were made in 1838, increasing yearly to a maximum of 4,784 in 1856 and decreasing to 1,672 in 1877 and fluctuating around the 1,000 mark from then to the 1890s, reaching a low of 494 in 1899. In the twentieth century the highest number of arrests, as a consequence of the introduction of the Criminal Law Amendment Act, was in 1912, with 1,067 detentions, and then the arrest figures gradually decrease to a low of 198 by 1919.

Prostitution was often the resort of the desperate in a country that offered limited opportunities to young women and where a change in economic circumstances, such as the loss of employment or desertion by a spouse or breadwinner, plunged many women into economic crisis. Evidence from the Poor Inquiry of 1836 suggests that unmarried mothers who could not get the fathers to support them and the children were 'in some instances driven ... to prostitution as a mode of support'. Susanna Price took to prostitution and crime to support herself when her soldier husband was overseas. In 1840 she was sentenced to seven years' transportation for larceny. Catherine Grady, 'a notoriously improper character and public nuisance', pleaded guilty to theft in 1846 and was transported for seven years. A newspaper reporter commented that it was a 'happy riddance for the city'. Bridget Hayes, who was transported for larceny in 1848, pleaded that she had been seduced by a young man who cast her off and that she 'had to pursue a wicked life to keep herself from starvation'. Prostitutes were most often charged with theft, being drunk and disorderly, vagrancy and sometimes murder.[1]

Maria Luddy in her study of prostitution in nineteenth-century Ireland noted that some of the descriptions for prostitutes included: 'women of bad or abandoned character', 'unfortunate women', 'dirty persons', 'destitute women', 'night walkers', 'nymphs of the street', 'fallen women', and 'frowsy, shameless women'. The descriptions also give some insight into the general attitude of society towards them.[2]

Grafton Street, *c.* 1900. (Courtesy of Fotofinish)

The DMP figures suggest that there were 1,630 prostitutes in Dublin in 1838; by 1890 that figure had declined to 436. In 1922 there were 200 prostitutes in the Monto area of Dublin, according to Frank Duff, founder of the Legion of Mary; that number had reduced to forty by 1925.

A number of women worked in brothels, though they did not necessarily live in these establishments. Brothels, were recorded in police statistics as of either a 'superior' ('flash houses') or 'inferior' ('kips') type. In 1842 there were 1,287 brothels in Dublin. During the Famine years the number of brothels in the city hovered between 330 and 419, with in excess of 1,300 women working from them. By the end of the century, these figures had barely changed. The police were slow to close down brothels, believing that this spread the problem into new areas by dispersing the women.[3]

FROM BENBURB STREET TO PORTOBELLO

As we have seen, the notorious red-light district of Monto, located between Amiens Street and Lower Gardiner Street, which thrived between around 1860 and 1925, was not the first brothel area in Dublin. Hell was infamous and notorious in Europe in the eighteenth century. And in the first half of the nineteenth century, brothel-keeping and street-walking flourished in various different parts of the city.

Barrack Street near the Royal Barracks (now Collins) on Dublin's North Quays was a very popular meeting place for soldiers and prostitutes. Barrack Street has since been renamed Benburb Street in order to rid it of its disreputable history.

In an 1837 periodical called the *United Service Journal*, there was a piece about the area around the Royal Barracks (widely known as 'the Barracks'). The publication noted that 'scenes of riot, drunkenness and gross indecency' were commonplace, and that the area was home to many prostitutes but lacking in 'persons of decent and moral habits'.

Benburb Street (formerly Barrack Street) in the early 1940s. It was a notorious brothel and prostitute area in the nineteenth century because of the nearby Royal Barracks. (Courtesy of GCI)

The article pointed out that the Royal Barracks has long been cursed with:

> ... a line of brothels and low public-houses called Barrack-street, and filled with the most abandoned crew of rogues and prostitutes. Dens of filth and iniquity, every kind of disease was engendered and propagated, and every description of crime contrived and encouraged. The troops in the Royal Barracks have constantly been injured in comfort and health, in conduct and discipline, by this sink of physical and moral contamination. Scenes of riot, drunkenness and gross indecency there exhibited, even in the open day.[4]

The area near Stephen's Green, including York Street, Mercier Street and Cuffe Street, was also a locality with many 'disorderly houses'. Mercier Street was originally called French Street, but following a number of police raids which closed the brothels, the city authorities changed its name. Lincoln Place at the Merrion Square end of Trinity College was another den of iniquity. In 1862 the authorities changed its name from Park Street to its present name. Nearer Monto, Temple Street was renamed Hill Street in 1886, again because of the brothels in the area.

The Portobello area of Dublin, located between the South Circular Road and the Grand Canal, was also notorious. This area was wedged between two important barracks: Portobello Barracks, stretching between Rathmines and the Grand Canal (now Cathal Brugha Barracks), and Wellington Barracks (later Griffith Barracks/Griffith College Dublin), near Leonard's Corner.

Morgan's Place, near Benburb Street and the Four Courts, 1948. In the nineteenth century and again in the later twentieth century, this area was a notorious prostitution centre. (Courtesy of Archiseek)

Grafton Street, 1888. This was a favourite walking area for Monto prostitutes.
(Courtesy of Dublin Forums/Cosmo)

The original name of Victoria Street in Portobello was Kingsland
Park. It was developed from 1865 onwards by Frederick Stokes,
a major Dublin property developer. Some of the houses in this
street stood empty for some time after they were built and came
to be frequented by 'ladies of the night' who 'catered to the nearby
barracks'. As a result the street acquired a bad reputation and
respectable families moved out. Even after the street ladies moved
on, the bad reputation remained, and eventually the name was
changed to Victoria Street. For a similar reason, Liverpool Road
became Portobello Road and Bloomfield Place/Rosanna Place
became Windsor Terrace.[5]

Towards the end of the nineteenth century, the long-time
link between soldiers and prostitutes ensured that places like
Barrack Street, Portobello Road, Mary's Lane behind the Four
Courts, Moore Street, Henrietta Street, French Street (Mercier) and
Purdon Street (between Mecklenburgh and Montgomery Streets)
were areas notorious for thriving prostitution.

THE CURRAGH WRENS

For many prostitutes, the army barracks was the honeypot to which they gravitated. Just outside Dublin, another barracks, the Curragh Camp in County Kildare, like so many military garrisons in Ireland at the time, had a particular problem with prostitution and was mentioned in the Contagious Disease Acts of the 1860s, which allowed the authorities to stop and arrest women if they suspected them of being prostitutes. In the furze-covered areas surrounding the barracks, approximately sixty women, mainly prostitutes, initially set up camp in what were known as 'nests'. These women became known as the 'wrens'. Their story gained prominence in a series of articles in the *Pall Mall Gazette* by the English journalist James Greenwood in 1867. His book, *The Seven Curses of London*, also contains a chapter on the Wrens. Following his visit to Kildare, he published a harrowing description of the condition of the women and, in the following year, when the Curragh of Kildare Act was passed it enabled the authorities to take action to regulate the use of the plains.[6]

The following is an excerpt from one of his articles:

The visitor found that there were ten 'nests' in all, accommodating about sixty women aged between 17 and 25, some of whom had been there for up to nine years. Located in a clump of furze, and known by a number given to it by the inmates – who numbered from three to eight, each nest consisted of a shelter measuring some 9'x7' and 4'/2' high, made of sods and gorse. With a low door, and no window or chimney, and with an earthen floor, the 'nest' had for furniture a shelf to hold a teapot, crockery, a candle, and a box in which the women kept their few possessions. Upturned saucepans were used as stools, and the straw for bedding was pushed to one side during the day. At night the fire within the shelter was covered with a perforated pot, and the women undressed to sleep in the straw. In summertime the 'nests' gave some shelter, but in winter the wind whistled through them.

The women, who were all Irish, came from different parts of the country. Some of them had followed a soldier from another station; others came to seek a former lover, while the majority sought to make a livelihood. They lived, received their families, gave birth and died in the 'nests'. Their clothing consisted of a frieze skirt with nothing on top except another frieze around the shoulders. In the evenings when the younger women went to meet the soldiers, in the uninhabited gorse patches, they dressed up in crinolines, petticoats and shoes and stockings. The older women remained behind to mind the children, of whom the visitor counted four, and to prepare food. All the takings of a 'nest' were pooled, and the diet of potatoes, bread and milk was purchased on the few days when the women were allowed to attend the market in the camp. Otherwise it was out-of-bounds, but an army water-wagon brought them in a regular supply. While the hospital in the camp catered for soldiers, and where it was estimated many of the patients suffered from VD, there was no medical aid for the women except in Kildare infirmary, or Naas workhouse and jail. Doctors did not come to the 'nests'. The gentleman from the *Pall Mall Gazette* decided that, contrary to popular opinion, the women did not live in the furze because they loved vice. They were there because it was known that those who sought refuge in the workhouse at Naas lived in even worse conditions.

The 'Curragh Wrens' were there because there was a demand for them from the soldiers, and 500 such women were estimated to be in the locality in 1865.[7]

The Prince of Wales, later King Edward VII, was introduced to an actress, Nellie Clifden, while he was based at the Curragh Camp. She was smuggled in by his fellow officers. He was at the Curragh, in 1865, 1868, 1871 and 1885.

Much of the prostitution in Dublin, Kildare and elsewhere was fuelled by the expanded military presence in Ireland; there were up to 30,000 soldiers stationed around the country most of the time. As the nineteenth century progressed, prostitution in Dublin became more geographically confined. After the 1870s

A contemporary illustration of when Edward, the Prince of Wales visited the slums of Dublin, 1885. He was also renowned as a frequent visitor to Monto. (Courtesy of Dublin Forums/jembo)

women began to move into cheaper accommodation available in the Lower Mecklenburgh Street area. The evidence of the Rev. Robert Conlan to a commission on housing in 1885 revealed that brothels were extending into the district. He observed that some of the houses were 'regular bad houses', but that in the case of tenement houses 'bad people who would carry on the same trade would take a flat', so that brothels in this area were now to be found in tenement houses that also contained respectable families. Mecklenburg Street was beside Montgomery Street, a similar Georgian-designed street, and was populated with similar people and activities. It was Montgomery Street that gave us the name Monto.[8]

A PLACE CALLED MONTO

The Monto area, a mere square mile of streets, was within that part of Dublin bounded by Talbot Street, Amiens Street, Buckingham Street, Sean McDermott Street (formerly Gloucester Street) and Lower Gardiner Street. The Monto name derived from the street near Amiens Street (Connolly) railway station called Montgomery Street (now Foley Street), which runs parallel to Talbot Street. Montgomery Street was named after Elizabeth Montgomery, who married Luke Gardiner, Lord Mountjoy, who had laid out many of the fine streets in the area. Some of the few names that have survived from the Monto era include Beaver Street and Mabbot Lane. Bella Street and Bella Avenue, off Buckingham Street, are named after the madam of them all – Bella Cohen.

At one time the district was very fashionable with many grand houses. And that was why the first madam of Monto, Moll Hall, chose the area – she had social ambitions. The renowned architect James Gandon lived in Mecklenburg Street in the 1840s, according to *Thom's Directory*, and some solicitors had their offices here.

This street was composed of two-, three- and four-storey Georgian houses. The upper end of Mecklenburg Street, even in Monto's heyday during the latter decades of the nineteenth

Example of a late Victorian prostitute to be found in the 'flash houses' of Monto.
(Courtesy of GCI/harvest)

century and up until 1925 in the twentieth century, had a certain seedy respectability, containing only a few brothels for the wealthy. Most of the brothels were in the lower end of the street. The brothels were in crumbling Georgian houses, often right next door to respectable local working-class dwellings where dockers, labourers, dressmakers, laundresses, carpenters, grocers, fishmongers and carters lived. In 1885, a local mother wrote to the *Freeman's Journal* begging the authorities to suppress the prostitution in her area. She criticised the 'obscene language' and 'indecent conduct' of the 'abandoned women who crowd our streets nightly, and ply their trade without the slightest attempts at concealment'.[1]

By 1887 the street had dramatically deteriorated, both physically and in reputation, and Dublin Corporation changed the name to Tyrone Street in an attempt to hide its growing and terrible reputation. But the problem did not go away, and in 1911 Dublin

A bustling Eden Quay at O'Connell Bridge at turn of the nineteenth century. (Courtesy GCI)

Men working at the junction of Gardiner Street and Dorset Street, *c.* 1913, laying a drainage pipe. On the building on the left can be seen a statue holding three balls – symbol of a pawn shop, an important place for the working-class Dubliner in the Monto/Summerhill area. (Courtesy of DCC)

Corporation, in another failed attempt at change, renamed it Railway Street, its present name.

Halliday Sutherland recalled that in 1904, as a medical student in Dublin, he had walked one evening down Tyrone Street. He observed: 'in no other capital of Europe have I seen its equal. It was a street of Georgian houses and each one was a brothel. On the steps of every house women and girls dressed in everything from evening dress to a nightdress stood or sat.'[2]

The area was notorious in the closing decades of the nineteenth century and the beginning of the twentieth-century not only for the audacity of the unregulated – but not illegal – prostitution found there, but also for its shocking levels of poverty. It was a rough place where 'dog ate dog'; dockers, railwaymen, coalmen, carters, domestics, factory workers and all sorts lived side by side in a melting pot of tenements, with pubs and brothels on every side of them, and the police dared not enter.

This square mile or so of streets, lanes and narrow squalid alleys of Monto was the den of brawny madams and brothels that catered for, amongst its many customers, soldiers and sailors that came from the wild, dangerous, adventurous and colourful life of the seafaring and military cultures. The Monto district, a stone's throw from the Custom House and the capital's Sackville Street, welcomed the thousands of soldiers based in Dublin's main barracks'. Monto was also a sailor's stroll from the teeming Dublin docks where ships unloaded their commercial cargoes and their lustful crews. For these soldiers and sailors knew, by experience and reputation, that Monto was justifiably regarded as Europe's biggest and boldest red-light district. It had a certain whiff of mystery, magic, adventure, glamour and danger, with the promise of unlimited sex and drink, where there was all-night carousing, gambling, music and song. Moreover, its location, near the Docks, the railway station and Dublin's main thoroughfare, meant that it was easy for visitors to get in to and out of.[3]

Moll (Mary) Hall operated her brothel in Mecklenburgh Street from the late eighteenth century; she was joined later by another madam, Mary Crosby. By 1837 the area was noted for its 'great number of destitute poor, [and] dissolute and depraved characters' of both sexes. Respectable families moved out, and the madams moved seamlessly into the deteriorating houses. These were joined by the many pubs and shebeens that sprung up, all providing visitors with music and singing, entertainment, gambling, joviality, girls and endless after-hours drinking. The raucous pubs and brothels of Monto were packed every night with drunken revellers, many of whom never stayed sober long

The end of an era. View of the Gloucester Diamond in 1980, prior to demolition. (Courtesy of Dublin Forums)

enough to recall the precise details of their visit. Nearly every house held a brothel and nearly every doorway had a prostitute displaying her wares. These brothels lurked in a squalid poverty-stricken slum of streets. They were like any other back streets in a Victorian era city – though by day, perhaps, a little quieter and a little more deserted with windows of tenements shuttered and curtained, desultory children playing, a sailor or two looking lost and sheepish and perhaps a well-dressed gentleman scurrying towards the better part of town. This is where one would see a Tommy or navvy vomiting into a gutter, redcoats carousing, students prowling around, fighting and brawling; where one would hear drunken singing, music and laughter. This was Monto in its heyday.

Throughout the nineteenth century and early twentieth century, until the 1920s the red-light district of Monto not only prospered but was renowned among soldiers, seamen, medical students, politicians, race-goers, rural cattle dealers, newspaper reporters – all and sundry, in fact. Drinking and prostitution was tolerated on a twenty-four-hour basis. Anyone could open a brothel, and this was compounded by the very important fact that there was no legislation in Ireland outlawing the burgeoning business.[4]

Two young girls from Monto area, going to get milk or water in the jug carried by one of them, *c.* 1900. (Courtesy of UCC)

WORLD'S END:
THE STREETS OF MONTO

AMIENS STREET

Before we progress, let us look at some of the principal streets of this famous and colourful area of Dublin. The writings of Charles Dickens, and his criticism of social injustices, found an influence on the place-names of Monto with Nickleby Place for instance being called after *Nicholas Nickleby*, one of his major novels in the middle of the nineteenth century. Other famous names had an influence also. In 1728 Amiens Street was known as The Strand. In 1800 it was renamed Amiens Street after Viscount Amiens, who had been created Earl of Aldborough in 1777. The terminus of the Great Northern Railway was built on Amiens Street in the years 1844–46 to a design by William Dean Butler. It was later renamed Connolly Station, in memory of the 1916 Rising leader James Connolly. At the junction of Amiens Street and Portland Row is the famous Five Lamps, erected to the memory of General Henry Hall, who served with the British Army in India.

Across the road from the Five Lamps are Portland Row and the site of Aldborough House, which was filled with 3,000 soldiers in 1843 following Daniel O'Connell's call for a Monster Meeting at Clontarf. It did not start life as a barracks but was built in 1796 by Edward Stratford, Viscount Amiens and Second Earl of Aldborough as a residence. It was a fine Georgian structure and the last of the great townhouses of the period. It was the second largest Georgian private residence in Dublin, surpassed only by Leinster House. Described by An Taisce (the National Trust of Ireland) as the last great town mansion built before the Act of Union, it has a tall, three-storey central block flanked by quadrants which led to pavilions – one with a chapel and the other with a private theatre. Its first owner died within three years of its completion. His widow remarried but died eighteenth months after her first husband. Years of legal wrangling followed. Subsequently the house was rented to a Professor Gregor Von Feinagle, a Cistercian educationalist, for his Feinaglian School. Following the closure of the school the army used it periodically, and this was one of the reasons why prostitution flourished in the adjacent streets of Monto.[1]

The Five Lamps, Amiens Street, near Monto, in the late 1950s. (Courtesy of GCI)

Early architect's plan for Amiens Street railway station. (Courtesy of Archiseek)

Early nineteenth-century print of Aldborough House, later Barracks, at Portland Row, overlooking the area of Dublin called Monto. (Courtesy of Fotofinish)

BUCKINGHAM STREET

Near the Five Lamps we have Buckingham Street. This street was named after a Viceroy, the Marques of Buckingham. Laid out as an ambitious speculative development in 1788, the new, wide thoroughfare of Buckingham Street was intended to be as elegant a street as any in London. However, following the Act of Union which took effect in 1801, transferring the seat of government from Dublin to Westminster, the city experienced a serious decline in political and economic fortunes. Property prices fell dramatically, and the area, like many of the surrounding streets and houses of Monto, went into rapid decline, and the fine houses, like everywhere in Monto, became sagging tenements.

Dublin tenements in the first decade of the twentieth century. A collection of hats and coats can be seen for sale at a second-hand market in Horseman Row, Parnell Street. (Courtesy of GCI)

Foley Street, 1940. (Courtesy of Irish Volunteers Commemorative Committee)

No. 36 Buckingham Street was once the home of John O'Donovan, the father of a family of Fenians. One of his sons, also called John, made rifles and bullets in this house. O'Donovan Rossa, James Stephens, Thomas Clarke and John Luby held Fenian Council meetings in the front parlour of this house. John O'Donovan was also a great scholar and translated many Gaelic manuscripts including the works of the Four Masters in 1864.[2]

MONGOMERY STREET/FOLEY STREET

Montgomery Street, as already noted, was named after Elizabeth Montgomery, who was married to Luke Gardiner, and it is from this street that the area takes its name. In earlier times it was known as World's End Lane, and later it would become Foley Street.

It was once a fine street of well-built and attractive Georgian houses. John Henry Foley, the sculptor responsible for the Daniel O'Connell Monument on O'Connell Street, once lived in Foley Street, hence the name. John Foley (1818-74) was one of the most successful sculptors in Ireland. He was born at no.6 Mecklenburgh Street. His father was a glass-blower and grandfather a sculptor. The O'Connell statue was regarded by Foley as the crowning glory of a very illustrious career in Ireland and Britain. However, he died before the work was complete but it was

Family life in Buckingham Street, 1940s. (Courtesy of Dublin Forums)

Foley Street/Corporation Street junction, 1940. (Courtesy of Archiseek)

eventually unveiled in 1882, to much acclaim. His other works included the statue of Henry Grattan on College Greet, Benjamin Guinness in the grounds of St Patrick's Cathedral and Oliver Goldsmith and Edmund Burke, both in front of Trinity College Dublin. This long and narrow street between Amiens Street/ Buckingham Street and Lower Gardiner Street was the heart of the notorious red-light district for decades. Once a fashionable part of Dublin, the street suffered from serious decline in the nineteenth century, as the grand houses were converted into crowded tenement buildings.

From 1914–27 the corner of Foley Street and James Joyce Street (formerly Corporation Street) was occupied by Phil Shanahan's pub, renowned for its role as an important meeting place during the War of Independence. Other pubs still in existence from the heyday of Monto include Lloyds (1893) and John Mullet's, both on the corner of Foley Street and Amiens Street.[3] Foley Street to this day still retains its narrow, dark and forbidding appearance, despite much development and re-generation. The name 'Montgomery' lives on in an apartment complex.

GARDINER STREET LOWER

Gardiner Street is one of Dublin's best-known Georgian streets and marked the western end of Monto. This street was named after Luke Gardiner, Viscount Mountjoy, in 1795. The family

Gardiner Street, 1952. (Courtesy of Dublin Forums/Rashers)

Celebrating the 1932 Eucharistic Congress in Marlborough Street, looking towards Parnell Street not to far from the Monto area. (Courtesy of GCI)

A fire in a tenement house in Gardiner Street, 1938.
(Courtesy of Dublin Forums/jeangenie)

Ornamental
doorway on
Gardiner
Street, 1949.
(Courtesy of
Dublin Forums/
Damntheweather)

spanned three generations of builders and was a major landowner
in the north inner-city area. The family's presence was very
significant in the mid- to late eighteenth century and they introduced a new architectural form – the Georgian style which is now
synonymous with the city. The Gardiners' developed many parts
of the north city, including Gardiner Street, Mountjoy Square,
Buckingham Street and Summerhill. Gardiner's greatest achieve-
ment was to lay the basis for Dublin's premier street, first called
Gardiner's Mall, subsequently known as Sackville Street and
now of course O'Connell Street.[4]

Commenced in 1792 and finished around 1820, Gardiner Street
itself was developed by Luke Gardiner and for many years it

Sweep of fine Georgian houses on Gardiner Street/Summerhill in the 1960s.
(Courtesy of GCI)

Summerhill, 1953. (Courtesy of Dublin Forums/Rashers)

was one of Dublin's most fashionable streets with fine Georgian houses for the well-to-do lining both sides. Unfortunately, like so many of the dwellings in the nearby streets, Gardiner Street and the surrounding area's difficulties were further compounded and quickly deteriorated in the decades after the Act of Union, when 'the rich marched out and the poor marched in', according to a local saying.

Having a chat outside a Georgian house in Monto area, early 1940s.
(Courtesy Dublin Forums/Damntheweather/Mr Johnson)

Luke Gardiner the Second was killed while leading his regiment, the Dublin Militia, at the Battle of New Ross, County Wexford, during the 1798 United Irishmen Rebellion.

However, following his death, the Gardiner Estate was sold off in parcels to various owners, including the brothel-keepers of Monto. An example of the fate of the wider area is Gloucester Street, off Gardiner Street, which did not have a single tenement house in 1870; it was solidly tenement by 1900.[5]

The tenements lasted until well into the twentieth century but were demolished from the late 1940s onwards, and modern flats and apartment complexes constructed in their place. The Labour Exchange at the lower end of this street was built in 1838 as the Trinity church. It closed in recent decades and now operates as a venue for city events. There are a number of small hotels operating along this part of the street also. The Central Model School at Deverell Place, off Lower Gardiner Street, is over 150

Celebrating the Marian Year in Corporation Buildings, Corporation Street, 1954. (Courtesy of Dublin Forums)

years old. The *Irish Catholic* newspaper was published from here for over 100 years. The external wall clock is still working after all these years.

In May 2011 Britain's Queen Elizabeth II visited Gardiner Street and later joined Irish President Mary McAleese to lay wreaths at the Garden of Remembrance.

FAMOUS RESIDENTS

Former residents of the area included playwright, producer and actor Dion Boucicault (1820–1890) who lived in no. 47 Lower Gardiner Street (now The Townhouse Hotel). He was extraordinary and flamboyant and his plays reflect not only some of the pivotal events in Irish revolutionary history but also his unique

Moran's Hotel, at the junction of Gardiner Street and Talbot, was seized by the Irregulars during the Civil War. An attack by the Free State troops in which a field gun, mounted on a truck on the railway bridge, was used, forced them to evacuate. This picture shows one of the windows after the attack. (Courtesy of Dublin Forums/GCI)

The Yards, Summerhill, near Monto, 1960s. (Courtesy of GCI)

personality and style. Reflecting his lasting influence, some of his most popular plays include *The Shaughraun* and *The Colleen Bawn* are still shown from time to time at the Abbey Theatre.

Lafacadio Hearn (1850-1904), who lived next door at no. 48, became an international writer best known for his books about Japan, especially his collections of Japanese legends and ghost stories. He had moved to Japan in 1890 and it was there that he found his home and greatest inspiration. He offered the West some of its first glimpses and insights into pre-industrial Japan.[6]

RAILWAY STREET (MECKLENBURG STREET) AND MOLL HALL

Besides Montogomery Street, and running parallel to it was Mecklenburgh Street. The street was formerly called Great Martin's Lane, renamed Mecklenburg Street in 1733, and subsequently renamed Tyrone Street in 1887 and Railway Street in

1905. The name Mecklenburgh Street came from Charlotte Sophia, Princess of Mecklenburgh-Strelitz and wife of George III. At that time and in subsequent decades it was an area of fine houses and even finer well-to-do residents. However, by the middle of the nineteenth century, according to official figures, more than half the houses were classed as tenements. And with the decline of the area, the new owners of the houses did not mind whom their tenants were, provided they paid the rent. Some of these tenants were soldiers billeted there because of the shortage of room in the converted Aldborough House army barracks, facing the Five Lamps. With the arrival of the soldiers in the area, brothels sprung up along the street. From 1800 to 1900 it was said the area here and the adjoining streets contained some 1,600 prostitutes. Lower Mecklenburg Street was one of the most notorious of all the streets in Monto. Unlike Upper Mecklenburgh Street, where some of the nineteenth-century houses were well maintained by

Ruins and dilapidated buildings, Railway Street. This photograph is one of those taken by W.J. Joyce in 1913 to illustrate the dreadful living conditions in Dublin. Railway Street was originally called Lower Tyrone Street and was part of the notorious Monto area. (Courtesy of GCI/fotofinish)

the Monto madams catering for a wealthy clientele, the lower part of the street was full of decaying tenements filled with seedy brothels.[7]

Significantly, there is a link between Hell and this street. It was in this street at the end of the eighteenth century that Mary (Moll) Hall, a very close friend of Margaret Leeson (Pimping Peg), first set up her brothel, catering for the well-to-do. However, at this time the street was a sought-after location and highly respectable. At the close of the eighteenth century, another prostitute Mary Fagan (aka Mary Crosbie), a friend of Leeson's, also opened a brothel on this street, thanks to the purchase of a fine house for her by an ardent admirer, a Captain Misset. Thanks to Fagan, Misset ended up in the Debtor's Prison, having been robbed of everything by the prostitute, who continued to live a life of luxury. These well-off prostitutes were renowned in Dublin and dressed, dined and mixed with the top echelons of Dublin and Irish society. However, when Moll Hall suddenly became ill and was at death's door her creditors descended on Mecklenburg Street and cleared the house of everything she owned and left her dying on the floor surrounded by some of her girls. Margaret Leeson heard of her plight, but too late. However, she ensured Moll had a good wake with six coaches containing twenty-four prostitutes dressed as mourners. She also paid for a suitable headstone for the grave.[8]

Nearby, at Summerhill, there was another brothel at this time, run by a Mrs Wynne.

An interesting resident in Railway Street for a number of years was the infamous and legendary 'Gypsy Lee', the country's most famous fortune teller. Despite her fame and skills – in fact, possibly because of them – she was brought to court in the 1930s and charged with 'witchcraft and sorcery'.

Along Railway Street today, you will see the remains of a towering grey wall with huge imposing gates that constituted the rear of the Gloucester Street Laundry. This was a Magdalene Laundry, which ostensibly gave shelter and work

Nos 88 to 93 Railway Street. (Courtesy of GCI/fotofinish)

to 'fallen women' but conditions were harsh and the women exploited. It was through these gates that tons of laundry trundled everyday for the Magdalens to turn around as quickly as possible. The Magdalens were worked to the bone here. For example, the sheer weight of the very heavy irons the girls had to use was nothing like the lightweight version used in modern households. It required considerable strength to actually lift the iron before you started the back-breaking job of ironing huge sheets and everything else.

SEAN MCDERMOTT STREET (GLOUCESTER STREET)

Sean McDermott Street was originally called Gloucester Street, and received its present name in 1933. Gloucester Street (shown as Gloster Street on early maps) was named after William Henry,

Duke of Gloucester. The street was laid out in 1772. However, for much of the late nineteenth and early twentieth centuries the street was full of grim tenement houses. The poet Patrick Kavanagh spent his first night in Dublin in the late 1930s, staying in lodgings in Gloucester Street. According to the famous poet: 'I paid sixpence for my bed. There were six other beds in the room. The stink of that room has never left my nostrils.' And it has never left the memories of so many thousands of residents of Monto either, who, over the decades, were forced by circumstances to rear families in such a 'stink'.

The street is dominated by two buildings – the large Catholic church, Our Lady of Lourdes, built in 1954, and on the opposite side of the street the imposing and forbidding red-brick former convent and notorious Magdalen Laundry. The church holds a marble

Inside the Tin Chapel, Sean McDermott Street, 1950s. (Courtesy of Dublin Forums/rashers)

and glass memorial to the Venerable Matt Talbot (1856–1925), a reformed alcoholic who lived a very austere life. He is much revered in Dublin.[9]

The Gloucester Diamond got its name from the diamond-shaped intersection at Gloucester Place and Gloucester Street. Colloquially, The Diamond refers not just to Gloucester Place but to the entire area surrounding it. It is recorded on Thomas Campbell's map of 1811. The Diamond was located in the heart of Monto and thus of the city itself.

In 1941, Dublin Corporation bought Gloucester Place Upper and Lower, as well as surrounding tracts of land that included parts of Gardiner Street, Sean McDermott Street and Summerhill, by means of a Compulsory Purchase Order. Subsequently,

The famous '27 Steps', Gloucester Diamond. (Courtesy of North Inner City Folklore Project)

A view of the rear wall of Gloucester Diamond. Beyond it, the back of Georgian buildings can be seen. Many have windows with broken glass. (Courtesy of National Archives)

existing tenement dwellings were refurbished and demolished and new dwellings built, while cottages and smaller dwellings at Gloucester Place Upper were gradually cleared to make way for Lourdes House, built *c.* 1962, and Matt Talbot Court on Rutland Street Upper and Great Charles Street North (1972) and Mountain View Court on Summerhill (1977).

Following local developments, including protests and political deals – such as the famous Gregory Deal between politician Charles Haughey and local representative Tony Gregory – residents concerns regarding housing, education and employment in the area were soon pushed to the top of the central government's agenda. In the long run it led to more houses and improvements being initiated in Monto, not least the area around Gloucester Diamond.

The famous '27 Steps' from the Gloucester Diamond to Summerhill. (Courtesy of Dublin Forums)

27 Steps From the bottom

The street's diamond shape remains an enduring part of the topography today, while the old and memorable 'twenty-seven steps' that linked the Diamond with Summerhill survive in a modern format.[10]

The famous Irish sculptor, Thomas Farrell (1827-1900) was born in what was then called Mecklenburg Street. He also lived in Gloucester Street in later years (1851-1857) and nearby 30 Mountjoy Square. He followed in his father's footsteps and trained in his workshop and sculpture yard in Gloucester Street where he learned the craft and from where he worked for most of his career. He became the most successful sculptor in Ireland in the second half of the nineteenth century and his works are to be seen today throughout Ireland, but particularly in Dublin. He is responsible for

Monto children from Corporation Buildings, *c.* 1940. (Courtesy of GCI/harves/jeanjenie)

many of the statues we see around Dublin, including Lord Ardilaun and Robert Emmet in St Stephen's Green, John Grey and William Smith O'Brien in O'Connell Street. His work is also displayed in the Four Courts, Leinster Lawn and the Pro-Cathedral (Cardinal Cullen and Archbishop Murray). His works are also on display in Glasnevin Cemetery (e.g. the recumbent figure of Cadinal McCabe, the actor Barry Sullivan playing 'Hamlet' and members of the Irish Republican Brotherhood (IRB)).

STORE STREET

This street was designed by James Gandon for the merchants to house their stores after the building of the new Custom House. On one side of the short street is the city's main bus station, Bus Aras, an award-winning building dating from the 1950s and designed by the architect Michael Scott. No. 3 Store Street is the home of the Dublin City morgue. Store Street Garda Station

Shops and houses on Summerhill in the 1960s, before demolition. (Courtesy of Dublin Forums/archangel)

is one of the toughest and busiest in the city. The Dock Tavern (now Kate's Cottage), another pub in the Monto area, featured in Joyce's *Ulysses*.

TALBOT STREET LOWER (COPE STREET)

A mere short stroll from Dublin's O'Connell Street, and in previous times a gateway to Monto, this street was named after Charles Chetwynd, Third Earl of Talbot and Lord Lieutenant of Ireland 1817–21. It was formerly called Cope Street North. There are some striking and atmospheric pubs along the part of Talbot Street

Amiens Street railway station, *c.* 1900. Directly across the road from the station was the entrance to Monto. (Courtesy of GCI/harvest)

bordering Monto. Alfie Byrne (known as 'the shaking hand of Dublin') many-times Lord Mayor of Dublin was also a publican and purchased the Vernon Bar in 1912. Molloy's pub is a landmark 'olde-world' pub on the street. Grainger's is another noteworthy establishment. Mabbot Street (later Corporation Street and now James Joyce Street) linked Talbot Street to Railway Street and the very heart of Monto. Today, Mabbot Lane, connecting Talbot Street to Railway Street, is a reminder of one of the names from that era.

SOLDIERS AND SAILORS: DUBLIN, A GARRISON CITY

Besides the gradual decline of a once prosperous and fashionable area, there were other factors that would have helped create this notorious area called Monto. For centuries in Dublin, large numbers of regiments were coming and going from the wars in different parts of the expanding British Empire. After the 1798 Rebellion, the Act of Union of 1800, and the Robert Emmet Rebellion of 1803, more English soldiers were stationed in Ireland and this opened up opportunities for the expansion of the oldest profession in the world. The Crimean War, with thousands of troops billeted in Ireland (10,000 were based at the Curragh Camp alone), and general unrest in the country – Daniel O'Connell's Monster Meetings, the Young Irelanders of the 1840s, the Fenians and the Land Agitation of the closing decades of the nineteenth century – also necessitated having large numbers of soldiers being stationed in Ireland. The presence of so many prostitutes was determined, at least in part, by the significant military presence in the city.

The Royal Barracks (known as The Barracks and later called Collins Barracks) was the largest military barracks in Europe and dominated the northern quays overlooking the River Liffey near the entrance to the Phoenix Park. This barracks, founded in 1706 and taking forty years to build, was the most famous military school in the British Empire. A certain measure of relief was surely experienced by citizens when the barracks eventually opened as up to this soldiers were billeted with the people in the cramped confines of the walled old city. When the soldiers moved north of the river, with the building of new army barracks, so too did many taverns, bawdy houses and brothels. For many years soldiers from this barracks were some of the best customers of Hell, located further downriver and on the opposite banks of the River Liffey. However, from the nineteenth century, Monto's proximity to the Royal Barracks of the North Quays and Aldborough Barracks at Portland Row were key factors to its evolution.

The Boer War in the early years of the twentieth century and subsequently the First World War helped Monto business enormously as soldiers arrived at the various barracks in Dublin. Such was the number of soldiers arriving that there was shortage of accommodation in the barracks and the extra soldiers had to

Soldiers drilling in what is now McKee Barracks, Dublin, 1900. (Courtesy of Dublin Forums)

View of Aldborough Barracks from the Five Lamps, Amiens Street, 1960s.
(Courtesy of Dublin Forums)

be housed in Aldborough House on Portland Row, which was
converted to an army barracks housing 300 soldiers. However,
before the conversion was completed some of the soldiers were
initially billeted in lodging houses in Monto. It was an extraordinary stroke of luck for the brothels of Monto, bringing an influx
of customers to them, and the madams were quick to take advan-
tage. Furthermore, over the years the madams got to know the
movements of the various regiments and made a point of sending
their cards to the officers' messes.[1]

But it was not only soldiers that provided custom to the brothels
of Monto. Because of its close proximity to Dublin's port, droves
of sailors and seaman flocked to Monto when their ships docked.

Some of Monto's best customers. Lancers trooping past Trinity College Dublin, 1907. (Courtesy of UCC)

The madams, besides keeping track of the movement of new regiments to and from the various city barracks, also kept themselves abreast of new ships docking in Dublin. These ships would have been laden with nationalities from every corner of the world and having been at sea for weeks or months the sailors made straight for the renowned back streets of Monto and the ladies of the night. The madams had an organised system of messengers to get information from the Ballast Office in Dublin at the corner of Westmoreland Quay and O'Connell Bridge about the exact time a ship was expected to dock. The 1911 census showed the residents at no. 2 Faithful Place in Monto on a certain night of that year as two single women in their thirties and one Norwegian visitor, a 'seaman'.[2]

Moreover, the area's closeness to Amiens Street railway station (prostitution often thrived near railway stations throughout the world) did much to help business, as did the many farmers and cattlemen who came to the Dublin cattle markets from the country.

'THE WHORES WILL BE BUSY'

The many wars during the nineteenth and early twentieth centuries that Britain was engaged in saw much troop movement in Ireland as soldiers were despatched to battle or returned from the battlefields. The aforementioned Boer War of 1899–1901 was a case in point and its ending saw an increase in business in Monto. In fact, the *Irish Society* magazine in June 1901 printed a poem – signed J.R.S. of Knocklong but really by Oliver St John

British Troops inside Amiens Street railway station, *c.* 1920. (Courtesy of Irish Volunteers)

Gogarty, who had been a regular visitor to Monto when he was a medical student – pointing out this salient fact:

> The gallant Irish yeoman
> Home from the war has come,
> Each victory gained o'er foeman,
> Why should our bards be dumb?
>
> How shall we sing their praises?
> Or glory in their deeds,
> Renowned their worth amazes,
> Empire their prowess needs.
>
> So to Old Ireland's hearts and homes
> We welcome now our own brave boys.
> In cot and hall; 'neath lordly domes
> Love's heroes share once more our joys.
>
> Love in the Lord of all just now,
> Be he the husband, lover, son,
> Each dauntless soul recalls the vow
> By which not fame, but love was won.
>
> United now in fond embrace
> Salute with joy each well-loved face.
> Yeoman, in women's hearts you hold the place.

(Reproduced by kind permission of Ulick O'Connor)

Readers of the magazine, however, were quick to spot the scandalous message 'the whores will be busy', spelled out by the first letter of each line.[3]

Indeed they were, for by 1911 there were thousands of troops living in Dublin in at least eight barracks across the city. The Royal Barracks overlooking the quays could house nearly 5,000 soldiers.

At Richmond Barracks in Inchicore there was room for 1,600 soldiers, a hospital for 100 patients, officer accommodation and stabling for twenty-five horses. There was also Marlborough Barracks beside the Phoenix Park, Portobello Barracks and Wellington Barracks on the South Circular Road, and barracks at Islandbridge, Beggars Bush and Aldborough Barracks at Portland Row overlooking Monto. Mountjoy Barracks, the Magazine Fort, Royal Hospital (later Garda HQ) and St Bricin's – all were in the Phoenix Park. There were also soldiers housed at Pigeon House Fort, Dublin Castle, Loughlinstown Camp Field and Arbour Hill Barracks.

POVERTY AND PROSTITUTION

Dublin was not a busy industrial city. It had little in the way of major manufacturing, except stout (Guinness), biscuits (Jacobs)

Children outside tenement houses on Sean McDermott Street, 1940s. (Courtesy of Dublin Forums/Rashers)

and whiskey (Powers and Jameson), and therefore limited employment opportunities. Dublin had 26,000 families living in slums, the worst slums in Europe. And 20,000 of these families lived in one room each. Buckingham Street, in the heart of Monto, had sixteen houses in tenements according to the 1901 census. What is incredible and appalling is that these few houses held 499 inhabitants and this was the norm throughout the city. One observer who visited various tenements in the city recalled the depressing scenes:

> I entered a 'front-drawing room' on a sultry day in August. A child lay ill with whooping cough and was lying exhausted on the bed after a paroxysm [convulsion] of coughing. Flies were numerous in the room (it was a hot summer) and were passing and re-passing from the food on the table to the face and body of the sick child …

He also recalled a father:

> … who appealed to me, as one in temporary authority, to procure the ejection of a suspected 'unfortunate' from the room above his own. He said he was trying to 'bring up his children dacint [decent]' and how could he do it with women like that in the house.[4]

Because of bad housing, poor sanitation and bad diet there were major health problems in the tenements. The most common and dreaded of the 'killer diseases' was TB (tuberculosis) or 'galloping consumption', as it was commonly known because of the speed of its destructive effects. It was rampant and inflicted a high death toll on the poor because of their appalling living conditions. Diseases such as measles and whooping cough were highly contagious and very dangerous to undernourished children. Overcrowding and poor hygiene meant that disease was everywhere. Infant mortality was alarmingly high. Sir Charles Cameron, the Medical Inspector for Dublin, said: 'It is certain that infants perish from want of sufficient food.'

Typical family room in a Monto or Liberties tenement, 1913. (Courtesy of Dublin Forums)

Corporation Buildings, Corporation Street, 1954. (Courtesy of Dublin Forums/ Rashers)

About 20 per cent of all who died in the city (1,808 in 1911) were children less than a year old and nearly all of these deaths occurred among the poorest classes. Moreover, such was their poverty that the many pawnbrokers in the city were known as 'the bankers for the poor'.

The dreadful living conditions caused serious social problems. Alcohol played a very large role in the lives of many. It offered an easy escape from the dreary everyday troubles of life in the tenements. Workers who drank had little or no money to spend on their families. The problem was made worse by the custom, in some areas, of paying workers their wages in pubs. Crime was widespread in Dublin, and often connected with drunkenness. The figures for serious crimes – murder, rape and larceny – was one for every 100 people (higher than most large cities in Britain). It was not surprising then that there was a high rate of prostitution.[5]

Tenement children from Cumberland Street in the 1940s. (Courtesy of Dublin Forums/Damntheweather)

Long before a concerted effort was made to close down Monto's brothers (often described as the 'kips', in the early 1920s), the area had become a place of utter lawlessness, full of hellraising soldiers and sailors, bullies and 'fancy men', and young ladies strutting around in varying degrees and stages of undress, with streets and alleyways stinking of horse manure and alcohol.

THE MAN TRAP OF PURDON STREET

Even in the early decades of the nineteenth century Monto was establishing a reputation. *The Dublin City Name Book* of 1837 noted that Purdon Street in the heart of Monto was the location of an institution for worm complaints for the poor. The inhabitants of this squalid area included provision dealers, hucksters, labourers, destitute poor and 'dissolute and depraved characters of both sexes', according to the survey. From the 1860s onwards, during Monto's

Kelly's Row, off Gardiner Street, in the early 1940s. (Courtesy of Dublin Forums/ Damntheweather)

heyday, Purdon Street was known as 'a man trap', where street prostitutes lured men to be mugged by their fancy men. It was a street where there was no easy way out. The street lady would meet a customer in Jack Maher's pub on Purdon Street, and when he was filled with whiskey and stout she would lead him out and towards a gated laneway alongside the pub. Here, she or her pimp would most likely rob him and flee. Robbery, as well as prostitution, after-hours drinking and money-lending, was a major money-spinner in Monto.

There were many stories of cattle-dealers going to Monto after the various cattle marts in Dublin with their pockets full of money and being stripped of everything and being lucky enough to have their clothes to get away in. And if a victim caused a serious fuss over the robbery, he might just be caused to disappear and not a word would be said about it. There would be no truthful witnesses forthcoming if the police tracked the missing person to Monto.[6]

Monto brothels. Examples of former fine Georgian houses in Dublin that had become tenements and were later used as brothels. (Courtesy of GCI)

Halloween in Foley Street, 1953. (Courtesy of Dublin Forums/Rashers)

Many of the brothels were in dwellings ranging from the four-storey houses in Mecklenburgh Street to the single-storey houses and cottages in Elliott Place, Faithful Place or Beaver Street. It was an area of debauchery, vice and crime. Tenement houses, pawnshops, pubs, shebeens, cellars and secret passages, brothels, decaying buildings, dampness, filth and smells – all were part of the magic, mystery and horror of this mayhem. By the time Monto was closed down in the mid-1920s, however, much of the area had deteriorated even further, with many buildings in a ruinous state, deserted and abandoned. The former opulent, well-located 'flash houses' on Mecklenburgh Street were no more and the brothels were confined to the Purdon Street areas and the adjacent lanes and alleyways.

FLASH HOUSES AND KIPS: THE MADAMS

In nineteenth-century Dublin, and continuing right through to the 1920s, discretion was not strong enough to describe the blind eye that was turned to Dublin's booming sex trade that was located in Monto. Barely a few blocks in extent, and situated in the heart of Dublin's northern inner city, Monto was so well known as a centre for late-night drinking and prostitution that it even rated a mention in the 1903 (tenth) edition of the *Encyclopaedia Britannica*: 'Dublin furnishes an exception to the usual practice in the UK. In that city the police permit "open houses" confined to one street; but carried on more publicly than even in the south of Europe or in Algeria.'

Monto was also known as 'the Kips', 'the Digs', 'the Village' and 'the bad area' and sometimes as 'Hell's Gates'. In its heyday from the 1860s to the 1920s, there were anything up to 1,600 prostitutes working there at any one time, with all classes of customers catered for. It was reputed to be the biggest red-light district in Europe at the time.

Visitors who availed of its illicit, if hardly concealed, pleasures included famous literary figures such as James Joyce and Oliver St John Gogarty. Indeed, all classes of people were catered for – including wealthy professionals and indeed royalty, not to mention a Prince of Wales, who later returned as King

Edward VII. He would have been entertained with music and wine in downstairs parlour rooms in the plusher Georgian residencies. Before he became king and for years afterwards he was widely known as a philanderer and playboy. He had a very amiable personality and was a very popular figure. His forays into Monto are the stuff of legend in the local Monto community to this day. He would have accessed Monto through some of the secret tunnels that were dotted all over Monto, and was a frequent visitor there over a period of time. Years later, when the builders were demolishing the old tenement houses and cottages in the area, they came across Monto's infamous secret underground tunnels and passages. One of the passageways discovered ran in the direction of the Custom House. Part of the tunnel was discovered near Talbot Street during building and

A bustling Eden Quay at O'Connell Bridge at turn of the nineteenth century. Monto is behind the Customs House in the distance. There was a secret underground passage linking the Customs House to Monto used by VIPs. (Courtesy GCI)

road repair excavations as well as construction work in Monto itself.

Monto was a veritable haven of brothels, with multiple 'disorderly houses' or 'houses of ill repute' side by side. The brothels were in a number of categories, catering for different classes and depending on how much one was willing or able to pay.

The better class of brothel, further up Mecklenburg Street were called 'flash houses' and catered for the well-to-do, the nobility, wealthy merchants, sea captains and those in the higher echelons of society, whether Irish or English. This was where the houses retained some of their elegance and the prostitutes were fashionably attired and were visited regularly by their couturier. These first-class establishments had an atmosphere of style and prosperity, comfortably furnished and carpeted with plenty of flower arrangements, mirrors and lamps everywhere, elaborate wallpaper, and any number of private rooms. Music and dancing would be part of the entertainment. Customers of these houses would be greeted by well-dressed girls including many in full evening dress and would be warmed by coal fires blazing in the grates of the various rooms. Any customer would have to knock on the front door to gain entry, the exception made for very rich and high-profile customers who would gain entry via a secret passage. Naturally, the clients would pay dearly for the services of the 'flash houses'. First, there would be the entry fee, and then payment would be required for the obligatory extras including alcohol and the services of the girl. Alcohol itself was sold at exorbitant prices. And there was 'no change given in a decent house', according to one of the madams, Mrs Mack. The entry charge was 10 shillings, with an extra £5 for alcohol and sex.

Flash houses on Mecklenburgh Street (now Railway Street) were patronised by politicians and the gentry who patronised them after dark and who arrived in curtained cabs or motor cars. Some of these were the very cream of Irish and English society.

At a lower level there were those brothels that catered for ordinary businessmen, bank staff, newspaper people,

An example of a Victorian prostitute that could be found in the 'flash houses' of Monto. (Courtesy of GCI/harvest)

and members of the lower middle classes. These establishments operated mainly in Mabbot Street and Faithful Place, and often only wore raincoats which they flicked open occasionally to stimulate trade. James Joyce's biographer Richard Ellmann noted of these latter brothels that 'these houses were full of religious pictures behind which the ladies kept coshes of lead piping to prevent trouble'.

Then there was the lowest level of brothels, which catered for soldiers, sailors, students, labourers and general workers. Here the women and girls stood or sat on the steps of the brothels, enticing potential customers with teasing and flirting girls, whatever the weather.[1]

The side streets and lanes off Mecklenburgh Street housed these second- and third-class brothels, of a lesser standard and consequently cheaper for owner and patron alike. These

Grafton Street in the late nineteenth century – a happy hunting ground for Monto ladies. (Courtesy of GCI)

included Montgomery Street (Foley Street), Mabbot Street (James Joyce Street) and Lane, Beaver Street, Purdon Street, Elliott Place, Faithful Place, Uxbridge and Nickleby. These lesser quality establishments would have no luxuries. Linoleum replaced carpets and turf replaced coal. In some of the disorderly houses, there was no floor covering. Furthermore, clients were liable to be robbed, either by the girls or by the 'fancy men' or bullies (pimps) on the orders of the madams. The girl's pimp would rush in, grab the unfortunate customer, whack him on the head, empty his pockets and unceremoniously toss him out on to cobblestones of the dark street. A former bully boy, reminiscing years later, recalled that one such victim had demanded a refund on his money, complaining that 'there was more bounce on a bog', 'and with that we duffed up the aul sheep-shagger and gave him the heave-ho'! This was a regular occurrence. These girls would have picked up their customers in Sackville Street (O'Connell Street), Grafton Street or in the Monto area itself.[2]

THE MADAMS

Madams such as Annie Mack, Bella Cohen and Meg Arnott were some of the most notorious brothel-owners in the late nineteenth century. They were succeeded by madams such as Mrs Meehan, Becky Cooper and May Oblong in the twentieth century. Some of the madams of Monto were larger-than-life characters. One owned thirteen brothels and was a formidable woman, both physically and in personality. She ruled her manageresses, girls and bullies with the proverbial rod of iron. They had come up the hard way, having been prostitutes themselves in earlier years. And the very renown and notoriety of Monto partly came from the reputation, ruthlessness and business acumen of these madams. They were quick to see opportunities for expansion and when a nearby property became vacant they were quick to rent or buy it. They ruled their district with skill, organising a self-regulating, hierarchy of services: the youngest, prettiest girls decorated genteel-style parlours for select clients on the nicer streets, leaving the older, careworn and often ill women of the back lanes to less choosy sailors and soldiers. And there was no shortage of girls – desperate poverty made for desperate decisions, with reports in famine times of families selling their young daughters to merciless madams for the price of a square meal. Madams minded their business well, currying favour with men of power and influence and keeping the forces of law and order at bay through bribery and free services. They also had 'fancy men', 'bullies' or pimps such as 'Crusher' Kelly, 'Dizzy' Johnston or Jem Plant (who was regarded as being mad) to protect their enterprises. And besides being brothel owners they also acted as major money-lenders in the area.[3]

There was a veritable fortress of brothels running from no. 82 to no. 85 on the north side of Lower Mecklenburgh Street and under roughly the same continuous occupancy from 1888 until 1905 according to *Thom's Directory*, which is a rich source of information on the history of the various brothels in the area. Many of the madams who owned and managed the Monto brothels were quite well-off, often owning quite a number of houses. They would have been middle-aged, well attired, bejewelled, imposing and strong personalities, and ladies with much experience in the prostitution business. Some of the Mecklenburgh Street madams, according to Maria Luddy in her study of nineteenth-century prostitution in Dublin, 'had carriages to drive about, and horses to ride; ladies dressed in the pink of fashion'.[4]

By 1886, the brothels at nos 82–5 Lower Mecklenburgh Street became the stronghold of Mrs Mack, Mrs Noble, Mrs Arnold, and Mrs Cohen. In 1886 the madams were eyeing up more properties. Annie Mack was involved with nos 1–4 and 39 Lower North Cumberland Street, nearby, with Mrs Arnott at no. 5 Lower North Cumberland Street. Ellen Cohen and Ellen Cannell were both located at no. 29 Upper North Cumberland Street, and Ellen Cannell was completing the sale of no. 81 Lower Mecklenburgh Street.

Today, one of the most infamous madams of Monto is remembered in the street names of Bella Street and Bella Avenue, just off Buckingham Street. In Joyce's *Ulysses*, the chapter called 'Circe' has Bella Cohen having her brothel among the houses at Mecklenburg/Upper Tyrone Street. Joyce depicts her girls along the lines of well-known prostitutes such as Becky Cooper and Fleury Crawford.

The madams were a disparate collection of ladies. Some were Dublin women; others come from elsewhere in Ireland; others still come from England and Scotland. Most of them were widows in their forties and fifties. They shared a common situation and a similar outlook. They were lodging house keepers who turned their profession into a lucrative business – it was three times more profitable to rent out rooms for prostitution than to 'respectable' tenants. The madams usually had a manageress run the brothels for them. Profits were generally divided threefold – one-third to the madam, one-third to the manageress and one-third to the girls. The profits generally derived from the traffic through the brothel, robbery, and the sale of alcohol.

There were also links with the army – Harry Cannell was a sergeant in the army Service Corps when he married Ellen Charlton in 1883; Lizzie Arnold's husband Leamington was stationed at the military barracks in Clonmel, Tipperary, when he married her. These were important and very useful connections for the madams and helped them to gain entry to various barracks' and leave their calling cards.

Each of these women had brushes with the law over the years – some much more serious than others. But in general they evaded the notice of the police more than did their girls, many of who were arrested and constantly in and out of court and prison. When the madams were arrested or questioned, it was not for running a brothel (hard to prove and not necessarily the object of prosecution) but for associated crimes such as selling porter or spirits without a licence, or causing disturbances with their late-night champagne parties. All – or at least most – had short fuses and were capable of strong-arming their way through a dispute. They may have been respectful to Joyce, Gogarty and their friends, but they will have made life hard for their girls – their direct sources of income.

More significantly, the names of the madams seem sometimes to have become brand names, held by whoever was running the particular address at any time. Annie McEachern retired to Scotland in the 1880s but her name, Annie Mack, lived on in the area; Margaret Noble remained constant as a presence but under a hatful of different names; Lizzie Arnold was a shadowy figure facilitating various activities but playing the role – on the surface

An example of late Victorian-era prostitutes who could be found in the 'flash houses' of Monto. (Courtesy of GCI/harvest)

at least – of an invisible actor; Ellen Cannell lived a riotous life over several years in the late 1870s and early 1880s.

There is doubtless much more that can be discovered about these disorderly ladies. But the overall picture is clear: they ran successful businesses until the authorities closed in on them in the early twentieth century, and the influence of their houses survive in Dublin's folklore to this day.[5]

MAY OBLONG:
QUEEN OF MONTO

Perhaps the most feared of all the madams was May Roberts, a tall and broad woman better known as Madam Oblong. She married a publican from Moore Street and ran a shop in Mabbot Street (later Corporation Street and now James Joyce Street). She was noted for her cameo ear rings and vivid make-up. You risked your life if you crossed swords with her – she always had a bacon knife near to hand. She was often seen being driven around Dublin in a pony and trap and dressed in all her finery. She featured in a ballad: 'Long ago when men were men and fancied May Oblong …'

Life was brutal for many prostitutes and horrific punishments were meted out by May Oblong. If a girl said she had three customers but her pimp said more, she would be in trouble. Oblong slashed girls' faces and had some gang-raped by up to thirty men if they crossed her. For Oblong, 12 was the 'prime age' for prostitutes working in Monto and there was absolute uproar in Dublin when a child of these exact years was kidnapped and found in Monto. She worked her girls to the bone, and whatever the weather she would have them standing at street corners advertising themselves for business. And they would have to wait indefinitely until they had a customer. She also had her bullies watching the girls to make sure they stayed and looked for business.

MRS MACK OF MACKSTOWN

The infamous Mrs Mack, who appears in the 'Nighttown/Circe' episode of *Ulysses*, is recorded in the 1901 census as 50 years old, literate, Catholic, a widow and born in Cork city. Her five 'lodgers' were all female, literate and unmarried and ranged in age from 21 to 27. Two were Protestant and three Catholic, and they were born variously in Bristol, Woolwich, County Louth, Tullow and Limerick. They were listed as dressmaker, housekeeper, waitress, milliner and lace-maker (in other words, prostitutes). Also listed were a servant and a widow aged 32, who probably looked after the girls. Reputed to be an extremely greedy woman, Mrs Mack kept two houses, no. 85 and no. 90, on Mecklenburgh/Tyrone Street and half-a-dozen more elsewhere in the area, and was so well known that the whole area was sometimes called 'Mackstown', such was her influence and control in Monto.[6]

The medical students of Dublin had a bawdy song that began:

O there goes Mrs Mack;
She keeps a house of imprudence,
She keeps an old back parlour,
For us poxy medical students.

Oliver St John Gogarty was a fellow student (medicine in Trinity College Dublin) and friend of James Joyce and in his book, *Tumbling in the Hay*, described this famous madam as the owner of 'a brick-red face on which avarice was written like a hieroglyphic on the face of Mrs Mack and a laugh like a guffaw in hell'. Gogarty commented further on her distinctive face: 'Seen sideways, her straight forehead and nose were outraged by the line of her chin, which was undershot and out-thrust, with an extra projection on it, like the under-jaw of an old pike.' He also said, 'I thought of the grasping ways of her and her like ... She referred to her business as "a decent house" and the other brothels further up the street as "disorderly shanties".'[7]

Annie Mack's earliest address was no. 20 Lower Mecklenburgh
Street. It is noticeable that in 1874, several years before *Thom's
Directory* and the newspapers place her there, the house was
transferred on a forty-year lease by Patrick Gilmour to an Annie
McEachern. According to sale particulars nine years previously, this
might well have been regarded as a suitable purchase for a sumptuous
brothel. An advertisement in the *Freeman's Journal* during 1865
stated:

> Every portion of the House is in the most thorough state of repair,
> and nicely painted and decorated, and comprises two parlours, two
> drawing-rooms, several bedrooms, a good basement storey, and a small
> yard, &c. The lease includes the entire excellent Household Furniture,
> comprising a capital square London-made piano, mahogany, loo, card,
> dinner, breakfast and work tables; a prime spring stuffed sofa in hair-
> cloth; carved and gilt chimney and pier glasses; chimney ornaments,
> a nice lot of framed and glazed engravings; Brussels and Kidderminster
> carpets and hearth rugs; and a capital speaking parrot ...[8]

Oliver St Gogarty held the view of Mrs Mack as a grasping and
avaricious madam. But she was more than that. She was fined
from time to time for the sale of liquor but does not seem to have
been arrested for soliciting. That was not her game. She was the
brothel-keeper but did not solicit for business herself; it was
the prostitutes who used her rooms. In general the brothel-
keepers were in the business for profit alone. Mrs Mack was
a businesswoman who concerned herself with property deals
and with collecting money through the various houses she ran.
Mrs Mack dealt, like a businesswoman, with others in the same
or related businesses as her, notably Lizzie Arnold. She may
have been a hard woman to deal with, but perhaps she achieved
her aims. She may be distinguished from the more street-wise
Meg Arnott and likened more closely to the (apparently)
equally business-like Mrs Ellen (Bella) Cohen. In later years she
retired from running her brothels and concentrated instead on

selling dresses to the girls and being a money-lender. When she had acquired a substantial fortune, she retired to her native Scotland around 1889–90.

MORE MADAMS:
BELLA, LIZZIE, MAGGIE AND BECKY

Bella Cohen also found her way into world literature when James Joyce described her as 'a massive whoremistress' in *Ulysses*. At 228lbs she was considerably larger than most of the rather sylvan, lightweight prostitutes. By 1883 or '84 Bella Cohen (real name Ellen Cannell, *née* Charlton/Reece) had moved to no. 39 Lower Mecklenburgh Street, on the south side of Mecklenburgh Street and into the street in which Joyce places her – with Mrs Mack currently further back down the street at no. 20. She later moved to no. 82, which she occupied from 1888 to 1905. Mrs Cohen was often arrested up by the police for being

Hanging out the washing in the tenements of Monto in the early twentieth century. (Courtesy of Fotofinish)

drunk and disorderly and for damaging property. She remained in Monto till the early years of the twentieth century.[9]

Lizzie Arnold (aka Lizzie Leamington) was born Eliza McCarthy, and over the years she accumulated a portfolio of properties in the district. In 1890 she bought no. 40 Lower North Cumberland Street from Mrs Mack. She later made three further purchases from the same madam, who appeared to be divesting herself of her Dublin investments prior to her return to Scotland. She also had an interest in other properties in the area.

When Lizzie Arnold died in late 1915 she left a substantial portfolio of property. The Trustee's Sale after her death saw the following properties in Dublin sold: nos 17, 19, 21, 23, 25, 27, 27, 38, 40, 42, 44 Arnott Street, in the Portobello area of Dublin, business premises at nos 46 and 46a Arnott Street; a two-storey private house at 35 Whitworth Road, Drumcondra; and nos 40 and 41 Whitworth Road, Drumcondra.

Early image of Bella Cohen when she became a Madam of Monto. Lafayette Photographers, who took this image, were based at Dublin's O'Connell Bridge and were regarded as *the* photographers.

172

By making the best of her investments, and removing herself from Monto when business came under threat from the restrictions imposed by legislation and local clean-up schemes, Lizzie Arnold seems to have profited handsomely from her activities and in addition was able to stay living in the city of Dublin when so many of her colleagues retired abroad or elsewhere in Ireland.[10]

Margaret ('Meg', 'Maggie') Arnott ran another of the brothels along Mecklenburgh Street. She was frequently alluded to as one of Dublin's foremost madams, and was regarded as being the most elegant among them. Her maiden name was Higgins, and this may have influenced Joyce's choice of Zoe Higgins's name in *Ulysses*. Furthermore, the story of her life – as far as it is known – throws considerable light on what it was like to be a brothel-keeper in Monto at the end of the nineteenth century.

Nerney's Court, off Temple Street, near Monto, 1908. (Courtesy of Dublin Forums/jembo)

Unlike Mrs Mack the hard-nosed businesswoman, Meg Arnott was frequently in trouble with the civil authorities – more often than not in cases involving physical assault and the rough-and-tumble of northern inner-city Dublin streets. This is surprising, since she was barely over 5ft in height and a small build. To some extent she seems to have thrived on notoriety. She did not own a large property portfolio, but she was reputed to have made a financial success of the business she ran. She went under different names, depending on circumstances or court appearances – Higgins, Arnott, Noble, and La Touche. In one court appearance she admitted she ran 'an improper house'. Gogarty includes her in a list of prostitutes, madams and other street characters in his biography, *As I was going down Sackville Street*, along with Nora Seymour, Piano Mary, Dick Lynam, Becky Cunniam, Teasey (Teresa]) Ward, May Oblong, Mrs Mack and Liverpool Kate.[11]

Ulick O'Connor, in his *Oliver St John Gogarty: A Poet and his Times* (1963), noted: 'The madams were often women of intelligence. Meg Arnott, one of the most successful, lived in a mansion in Mount Merrion, and had a daughter at an expensive English convent school. On Saturdays, to increase custom, she drove her girls up Grafton Street in a landau.'[12]

She had had several brushes with the law. A *Freeman's Journal* report on one court case in late 1885:

On Thursday, 20th August, the officer was passing down Cumberland Street, and heard a great noise of music, dancing, and singing proceeding from the house of the defendant. Although it was between one and two o'clock in the morning, the place was brilliantly lighted up, and several showily attired girls were lolling about the door smoking cigarettes. The sergeant entered the house and found in elegantly furnished drawing room five or six young men and six or seven young girls, all more or less under the influence of liquor. On opening a cabinet in the room he discovered six full bottles of porter, and ongoing downstairs he found, on making a further search, a quantity of empty porter bottles and several glasses containing traces of fresh porter. There was also a bottle of whiskey concealed in a trunk. The defendant was absent, he was informed, and he believed she had since gone away to London.[13]

Two years later in 1887 she was again before the courts. According to the *Freeman's Journal*, 'A young woman of respectable appearance, named Maggie Arnott, residing in Mecklenburgh Street, was charged by a well-dressed man of the "masher" class, who gave his name as Ninian Wildridge Woods, MRCS, England, with having stolen a watch and chain value £7 10s, his property.'[14]

Ultimately life was not kind to Maggie Arnott. She was an Irish girl who had the sound sense to establish herself in a profitable business, but she did not seek to extend that business into an extensive portfolio of lodging houses or brothels like other madams. She was apparently of striking appearance, but quick-tempered, and perhaps her temper was her downfall. For medical or psychological reasons she was adjudged 'lunatic' at the time that her business faded around 1905. Her generation of lodging-house or madams was being disturbed by the authorities, and a new generation (including such ladies as May Oblong and Becky Cooper) was starting to take over.

A very strong character, Becky Cooper had a brothel in Mecklenburgh Street, in an excellent location, just opposite the Leinster Arms Pub. She was one of the most renowned prostitutes in early twentieth-century Dublin and the last of the madams that was present on that fateful day, 12 March 1925, when Monto was closed down. And she did not relinquish her chosen profession too easily and bargained heavily with Frank Duff and the Legion of Mary for a good financial deal to persuade her to retire. In her early career, at the turn of the twentieth century, she featured in a bawdy verse:

Italy's maids are fair to see,
And France's maids are willing,

But less expensive 'tis to me:
Becky's for a shilling.

She also owned a talking parrot. James Joyce had her in *Ulysses*, portrayed as Kitty Ricketts, a 'bony pallid whore …'. She ended her days living in Liberty House Flats in Railway Street. Here she was renowned for her loud and wild drinking habits in the pub across the road and visits to Jack Rafter's pawnbroker where she pawned anything she could in order to get the price of a drink.[15]

PIANO MARY AND LILY OF THE LAMPLIGHT: THE STREET WALKERS

The girls and women who worked for the madams in the brothels and on the streets were in many cases country girls fallen on hard times in the city, while the madams were mainly streetwise local women. For all the condemnation of their occupation, the girls were generally considered to be decent, unfortunate and kind, forced into a life on the streets through circumstance; quite a number ended up in penitentiaries or Magdalen Laundries like the one on Gloucester Street overlooking Monto. Prostitution for the girls was a terrible and tedious life, based totally on exploitation by the madams and the clients. Many times they were liable to cruel and degrading treatment including beatings by the madams, the 'bully boys' or 'fancy men' and drunken and callous customers. The younger ladies were generally pretty or handsome, well-dressed, and mostly didn't drink, whereas the more experienced ladies had a battered, downtrodden look to them from being on the streets every day for years. Traces of young beauty might still linger but their eyes would have a wretched and melancholic look. Attractive and once innocent and delicate figures would have grown emaciated and once luscious lips and mouths would now be hard and down-turned and covered in cheap paint. They aged long before their time. Many became perpetual drinkers, and some were clad in rags. Often, they would have made themselves deliberately drunk each day as a preparation for their street life. Black eyes, broken arms and dumped girls sleeping in doorways were a regular sight in Monto. All this was ignored by the authorities. Some prostitutes were even murdered, including Harriet Butler and Honor Bright.[1]

A study of the Dublin Police records in the late nineteenth century show that the vast majority of common prostitutes were poor, illiterate, aged between 20 and 30, and had a previous police record. Poverty forced many women into this: it was the only way they could get the money they badly needed. There was very little work for young women. Many ended up as domestic servants for the well-off. In the prosperous suburb of Rathmines alone there were 5,000 domestic servants looking after the well-heeled. Moreover, a girl of a tenement family (and there were thousands upon thousands of these) was forced to grow up quickly and was often a surrogate mother to her younger brothers and sisters.[2]

The population of working girls in Monto appears to be transient. The prison authorities kept records of the addresses at which they were born, in order to try to keep better track of their prisoners. Of course, the prostitutes and madams might easily give incorrect information to the authorities, sometimes impersonating other prostitutes. But despite this there does seem to be a strong thread of continuity. Girls (young and attractive-looking, who looked like they would be good money-earners for the brothels) were actively recruited by the madams, and dressed by them to make them better earners. Should they be arrested, their fines were paid for them. Many of these girls lived in lodging houses, either in Monto or elsewhere, including the Liberties. They would have to pay the madam for the rent of a bedroom for the night for themselves and extra for the customer.

These better-looking girls would not only have been dressed by the madams but also driven around on side-carts to Sackville Street to attract customers. Sackville Street (O'Connell Street),

Grafton Street and the Stephen's Green area near the Shelbourne Hotel were notorious areas for Monto prostitutes touting for business. Indeed, for many years, the custom in Sackville Street was that one side of the street was for 'respectable' people and the other side for prostitutes.

The girls worked in first-, second- or third-class brothels and also the shilling (very cheap) brothels. For them to work in the latter category meant that they were by this time diseased and their days working as prostitutes (or even staying alive) were numbered. The girls who worked in the first-class establishments, the 'flash houses', were very pretty, lived in the brothel and were dressed by the madams in the very height of current fashion. However, in the third-class establishments, the girls would just loiter and flirt with obvious intent on the steps of the brothels and entice prospective customers in.

Chancery Lane in the Liberties in the 1920s, close to where the Legion of Mary started their work. (Courtesy of Dublin Forums/ jeangenie)

Sackville Street (later re-named O'Connell Street) in the early twentieth century, during the heyday of Monto. (Courtesy of GCI)

The more attractive girls would also be despatched to the RDS for Horse Show Week, or to the races at Punchestown and Fairyhouse where they would mingle with the crowd and use their charms to flatter men and then bring them back to Monto with the help of speeding cabs. These best girls would also be sent, extremely well attired, to Grafton Street on a Saturday, again to encounter customers. Not only that, but the most attractive girls would be seen in the boxes of Dublin's premier theatres – the Theatre Royal and the Gaiety Theatre. Going to the opera and attending important balls in the Gresham Hotel, the Metropole Hotel on O'Connell Street or the Hibernian and Shelbourne Hotels in the Stephen's Green area, was all part of the work of the beautiful girls, who were always appropriately dressed for the occasion.[3]

Customers and girls making great haste from the RDS to Monto may well have been among this crowd of carriages. (Courtesy GCI/fotofinish)

Certain names of popular prostitutes have not been forgotten from the old days of Monto: Fresh Nellie, Connemara Maggie, Minnie Maypother, Fleury Crawford, Irish Nanny, Beautiful Nelly, Manchester May, Aida, Lottie L'Estrange who pushed a soldier into Spencer Dock, Cork Annie, Lady Limerick, Julia Rice, Aunt Betty or Lady Betty, Maggie Ballard, Meena La Bloom, Rosaline the Coalquay and the Goofy One, are just some of the names remembered. Piano Mary was another well-known prostitute. She acquired this name from a habit of running her fingers up and down the spine of a customer while they were in bed. Kitty D., a local girl, was regarded as a particular beauty with long, black hair down her back. She met and fell in love with a medical student. However, he was not happy with her way of life and one night brought her to his posh home on Fitzwilliam Square. Once inside the house he opened double doors leading to another room and in the middle of this room was an empty pine coffin. 'I'd rather see you dead in that coffin than see you leading the life you are leading', he said, and with that she ran screaming from the house. She gave up her ways and turned to religion and helping other ladies of the night change their ways too.[4]

Another figure in the area was Lily of the Lamp Light, so-called because it was her custom to always tout for business under a street lamp. And not just any street lamp. The lamp-post outside Jack Maher's pub on the corner of Corporation Street and Purdon Street was her favourite meeting place for custom. Other girls would sit on stools, depending on the weather, inside or outside Jack Maher's pub, as this was another well-known rendezvous for prostitutes and customers. When successful with a pick-up, they would take the man around the corner to the brothels in Elliott Street or Faithful Place. The area was full of pubs or shebeens that were also notorious for after-hours drinking.

These women did suffer. Oliver St Gogarty described one as having 'the remains of a beautiful woman'. Mrs Mack had scant respect for the ladies and called them 'doxies' and claimed their 'language would make me want to puke' and added that 'some of them would have the last word with their own echo'.[5] Their lives as prostitutes lasted no more than five years. They started off as

Faithful Place off Lower Tyrone Street in the heart of Monto, 1913.
(Courtesy of Dublin Forums)

fine, healthy and active but unemployed, like so many fresh young girls between the ages of 12 and 20 that swarmed the streets of Dublin. They made ripe pickings for the madams. Quickly any dream turned sour, and they became diseased, used, abused and tragic. They were quickly tossed back out onto the streets when their usefulness and money-making ability fizzled out.

Local activist and historian from Monto, Terry Fagan, who has written extensively on the area, interviewed many elderly men and women from the area. They recalled how the madams were despised by the uninvolved locals for exploiting those they referred to as the 'poor unfortunate girls', the vast majority of whom were country girls lured into the profession with the promise of initial housework. These 'unfortunates' also referred to the girls who became pregnant and were tossed out on the street by the madams. However, the local women looked after them and as they huddled and sheltered in tenement doorways brought them tea in 'tenement china', the name given for a jam jar of tea. Often the girls would leave their babies with the local women, promising to return. Most never did and these newborns were known as 'Monto babies'. Sometimes the mothers would return at Christmas and give out presents to the children.[6]

The question of debt was a terrible problem for the girls. All the girls, no matter what their earnings might be, were in debt. As well as having to pay for their accommodation, the very clothes on their backs were there on credit. The madams would keep the girls in debt, rent them the latest fashions and ditch them out onto the street when they became pregnant or, as Terry Fagan described it, 'when the effects of their lifestyle began to show ...'

THE LOCK HOSPITAL AND THE SWELL LADIES OF MONTO

Not only were most of the girls heavily in debt, but many of them were severely diseased. Venereal disease was rampant among the Monto

1872 image of nurses based in the notorious Lock Hospital. (Courtesy of Dublin Forums/Rashers)

prostitutes – and consequently among their customers. The problem of sexually transmitted diseases due to the prevalence of prostitution is evidenced by the Contagious Diseases Acts of the 1860s and 1880s. They were introduced as a direct result of the extent of venereal disease among the soldiers, and among their provisions was included forced medical examination of women. A lot of the women suffered from sexually transmitted diseases, and according to Terry Fagan they were often put out of their misery in the Westmoreland Lock Hospital for Incurables, Townsend Street, the favoured method of euthanasia being 'smotheration', he said.

The Lock Hospital – or, to give it its official name, the Hospital of St Margaret of Cortona – was situated on Townsend Street (the site is now occupied by *The Irish Times*). The Lock was founded in 1792 and opened for patients in 1794 and was one of the few establishments catering for venereal disease. Initially, the hospital treated 300 patients of both sexes. Later, its capacity was reduced to 150 beds and only women were admitted. The Lock – which was once described as a 'monument to moral degradation' – was more like a prison than a hospital. It was a dreary, monotonous and depressing place. Patients were made to wear drab clothing lest they offend the sensibilities of the governors of the hospital. Many of the patients came from Monto, as is shown by a witness to a government commission on Dublin hospitals who argued: 'If we allowed these swell ladies from Mecklenburgh Street to flit about in pink wrappers and so on, it would be a distinct inducement to others less hardened to persevere in that life (prostitution) in the hope that probably they would arrive at similar distinction.' However, once given some relief the prostitutes quickly returned to Monto. During the heyday of Monto venereal disease was rampant in the city and it was estimated that in 1880 over a third of the 5,000-strong Dublin garrison of the British Army was infected with it. In 1881 a British commander complained that half the unmarried men in his regiment had succumbed to venereal disease. Despite the obvious fact that prostitution was a huge industry in Dublin, the subject was rarely mentioned and the Lock was largely ignored by the public.[7]

LIKE A WITCHES' SABBATH

In the early 1920s, when Frank Duff of the Legion of Mary was engaging in his rescue work in Monto, he and other members of the Legion of Mary called at a brothel at no. 8 Elliott Street, off Railway Street, to try and rescue a prostitute by the name of Mary Kate. There were a number of young women in the house and in one of the rooms lay a dying prostitute. She was around 27 years of age, had been a prostitute for the previous nine years, and was now in terminal decline from venereal disease. Duff had her rushed to the Lock Hospital but she died a few weeks later. She was buried in Glasnevin Cemetery, as were many other Monto prostitutes. It was this concern for a dying prostitute that paved the way for Duff's eventual campaign to close down Monto.[8]

Frank Duff,
founder of the
Legion of Mary.

Another example of one who ended up in the Lock Hospital was Rose, a 16-year-old prostitute living in one of the Monto brothels. The harrowing way in which Rose met her death in 'The Lock' was typical of the fate of many of the young Monto prostitutes. Having contracted venereal disease she ended up in the hospital. There she was 'euphemised' (another local expression, meaning 'euthanised') by the nursing staff who were in the habit of smothering young women too far gone with venereal disease, after moving them to the end of the ward from which they could be silently evacuated at night without alerting the other diseased 'brassers'.

Subsequently Duff and the Legion visited the other brothels in Elliott Place trying to persuade the girls to give up their profession.

Duff was later to write of his experiences in Monto in a book called *Miracles on Tap* (the Archbishops of Dublin refused Duff permission to have his story published in book form in Ireland. It was eventually published in the USA in 1961. Duff was always regarded with much suspicion by the Church authorities partly because of the independent line he took). He was shocked at the 'spectacle of depravity' he saw in one of the Elliott Place brothels. On one occasion there was a bottle of methylated spirits ('meths') being passed around among the prostitutes who were standing in a circle. The girl passing around the bottle was standing inside the circle. She had given each girl two glasses. The larger glass was filled with water, the smaller one with the meths. The girls first drank the meths, then the water. The girls stood there, totally rigid, except for trembling hands, and with eyes staring and riveted on the course of the bottle of meths as it made its way around the circle. Duff likened the scene to a witches' sabbath ritual or dance. Red Biddy was another cheap and favourite drink for the ladies. This was a variant of cider and wine, often called 'mad-man's drink' such was its potency. These drinks were very popular because they were cheap and such was the power of their kick. Drinking water even hours later would revive the effects of the drink. One of the Monto ladies, Maggie Ballard, was known as the 'Queen of the Spunkers' and she had been over twenty years in the area. 'Spunk' was a slang expression at the time for methylated spirits.[9]

THE MURDER OF HONOR BRIGHT

Honour Bright (real name Lizzie O'Neill) was killed while working as a prostitute in 1925, and testimony at her trial showed that while the Monto area had gone quiet, some of the prostitutes had just moved elsewhere and business was still brisk outside the Shelbourne Hotel. Accounts of her trial also made it clear that the Dublin poor had a deal of sympathy for the 'unfortunate girls' working in their midst.

It was the Legion of Mary that first came across this tragic figure. The initial objective of the Legion of Mary was to visit impoverished women who were patients in the South Dublin Union Hospital in James's Street. One evening in 1922 Duff was visiting in Chancery Lane, off Bride Street, when by chance he entered no. 25, which was operating as a lodging house. This lodging house was occupied by a considerable number of prostitutes. They would not conduct their business there however. They would meet their customers elsewhere and take them up to Monto, where they rented rooms in the brothels. Among the girls in that house was Honor Bright. On a June night three years later Honor Bright, the single mother of a baby, was shot dead and dumped under a bush in Ticknock, in the Dublin Mountains, prompting a murder trial that was a *cause célèbre*

Chancery Lane, where Honor Bright had lodgings in 1925. (Courtesy of Dublin Forums/ martinb)

and became the talk of the country for months. She had worked in a clothing shop (Pyms) but when she became pregnant had lost her job. Circumstances forced her into prostitution and Monto. She had moved from Chancery Lane to another lodging house in Newmarket Street, the Coombe, at the time of her murder. A Garda Superintendent and a dispensary doctor were tried for her murder but acquitted. They had apparently met her and a friend in the vicinity of the Shelbourne Hotel and the girls were seen getting into the doctor's and Garda's cars. Speculation at the time suggested that the reason she was murdered was that Honor was going to name the father of her child. Following the murder, the Redemptorist Order priests gave one of their renowned hellfire and brimstone sermons in the Pro-Cathedral in Marlborough Street (near Monto) on the issue. Such was the horror and fear generated by the sermons that young ladies in the packed congregation were seen running screaming from the church.

There is a wall plaque at Ticknock, near Lamb Doyle's Pub, at the foothills of the Dublin Mountains, in memory of the murdered Honor Bright. Her family today are still committed to finding the truth about her tragic death.

Another prostitute, Harriet Butler, was murdered by a jealous admirer who shot her in the face.[10] That it took the jury just one minute to find the defendant not guilty has been the cause of much disquiet since.

THE MAGDALEN LAUNDRY – 'THE PENITENTIARY'

If Monto prostitutes were not murdered or beaten up they might end up in Mountjoy Jail or the Gloucester Street Laundry. Directly behind and overlooking the principal streets of Monto was this much-dreaded laundry. The deserted and stark red-brick building on what is now called Sean McDermott Street was a former convent and the adjacent laundry had served the Monto area since the late nineteenth century. It was built by the Sisters of

Our Lady of Charity and Refuge (the sign may still be seen over the entrance), which adjoins Railway Street, for former prostitutes to reform and do penance for their sins. Called the Gloucester Street Laundry it was known as 'the penitentiary' by locals. Girls who found themselves in 'trouble' were usually sent here instead of to Mountjoy Jail. 'Sent' is putting it mildly, for in fact they were 'shoved' in there, according to a local resident, the intention being to 'purify' or cure them of prostitution or other misdemeanours. The rescue and reform of prostitutes was seen as a major work of mercy by both the Protestant and Catholic Churches from the late eighteenth century onwards, but it took on added vigour from the mid-nineteenth century with the increase in the number of

Fundraising advertisement for Gloucester Street Laundry (aka Magdalen Asylum). (Courtesy of Fotofinish)

The Superioress and Sisters of

THE MAGDALEN ASYLUM, LOWER GLOUCESIER ST., DUBLIN

very earnestly beg the support of the liberal and kindhearted, to help them with the upkeep of the Institution for 130 Poor Penitents who receive a Home within its walls.

prostitutes in Dublin. The lay activists in these churches modelled themselves on Christ's dealings with Mary Magdalene in the Bible, so the prostitutes were called 'outcast women of society', 'fallen but penitent' or 'magdalens'. And there was a deliberate policy to locate the penitent asylums near or in the areas most used by the prostitutes.[11] Dublin's first penitent asylum was founded in 1765 at no. 8 Leeson Street, to help girls based in and near the areas of Hell and Stephen's Green. In 1830 another asylum was opened in Brown Street in the Liberties. Meanwhile, in the Monto area, in 1822 an asylum opened at 104 Gloucester Street, in 1833 at 76 Lower Mecklenburgh Street and in 1875 the Rescue Mission Home at 33 Lower Gardiner Street.

Michael McCarthy, in his book *Priests and People in Ireland* (1902), described the Magdalen laundries:

> It is a Magdalen Asylum, in which it is stated that there are penitents giving their service free until the 'nameless graves in the cemetery' claim their poor bodies. This Magdalen asylum [is] in Lower Gloucester Street, within the Mecklenburg Street area, in which there are 13 nuns who keep 90 fallen women at work at the profitable laundry business.

The demolition of parts of Monto over the years made way for the expansion of the Magdalen Laundry connected to the convent, offering some refuge to the women made homeless by the curtailment of their prostitution. The laundry continued in business until the end of the twentieth century.

It was only in October 1996 that the last of the laundries closed – the one in Monto. The overpowering stench of carbolic soap pervaded the building long after it closed.

On the same side of Sean McDermott Street as the convent and laundry, there is the front facade and the remnants of what looks like an ancient ruin with Greek lettering over the entrance. This is the former Scots Presbyterian church. Terry Fagan gave some interesting social insight on the church in an interview:

Well-off Dublin children in the 1930s, near Parliament Street and Capel Street Bridge. (Courtesy of GCI)

They helped the ladies of the night in the Monto area who wanted out from that life. They also ran a school across the road from the church which attracted a lot of poor children who went to get the free soup. In 1910 the bishop's built a school on Rutland Street to counteract the work of the 'free-soupers', as they were called. There was hand to hand fighting by different groups to prevent the children going to the Presbyterian school as they used to come home with anti-Catholic literature. This was like a red rag to a bull to the groups who marched on the school 'To save the souls of the Children'.

The school closed sometime in the late 1960s and the Presbyterian Church community moved to Howth, County Dublin.[12]

REGIMENTS MARCH OUT,
THE LEGION MARCHES IN

Many attempts had been made over the years to close Monto, but the authorities and police had consistently turned a blind eye to the problem. In the early years of the twentieth century, however, such was the persistent outcry in Dublin that the new Commissioner of the DMP, Sir John Ross, appointed in 1901, decided to tackle the problem once and for all. The issue of the sheer numbers

English soldiers leaving Dublin after the War of Independence, 1922. (Courtesy of GCI)

and audacity of the prostitutes had brought the issue to a head. Prostitutes from Monto looking for business paraded up and down Dublin's Sackville (O'Connell) and Grafton Streets, a short stroll from Monto, much to the horror and great annoyance of the public. Ross drew up a plan to close down this most notorious red-light district once and for all. His solution was for a number of organised raids by the police on the brothels in Monto. It was believed that such ongoing harassment of the madams and the brothels would greatly undermine the businesses and they would be forced to abandon the area and disperse. He did appear to have some success initially, as madams such as Bella Cohen and Maggie Arnott appeared to cease trading.

However, and in greater numbers, the prostitutes temporarily abandoned Monto but only to move on a more permanent basis to nearby Sackville Street, and the vicinity of the GPO. Here they continued their street-walking, met many soldiers and continued to provide their services in other houses in the city. Moreover, not only were soldiers being pursued for business by the prostitutes, but many shocked members of the public found themselves embroiled in the hubbub of a more noisy Sackville Street, full of prostitutes and soldiers and for probably the first time in their lives being called 'love' or 'duckey' or beckoned with 'psst, do you want to know something', 'did you hear', 'spare some time' or 'shilling for a blow' or 'do you want to go for a walk?' – being offered 'companionship' in return for a certain sum of money. In fact, the street was henceforth often considered impassable after 8 p.m. any night. Even the Archbishop of Dublin complained about the issue in a letter to the *Freeman's Journal*. He said in his travels around Europe he had never seen anything like Sackville Street, with all the soldiers and women congregating. A report in *The Irish Times* noted that the 'streets of Dublin are a reproach to us all. The immorality of Dublin is more public than elsewhere... all through the evening and well into the small hours of the morning; the streets are occupied by groups of girls who cannot possibly have reached sixteen years of age.'[1]

Dublin Corporation had tried to tackle Monto by changing the names of streets, but to no avail. It was told of the 'lewdness and immorality' of prostitutes stalking Dublin's main streets and congregating near the Custom House (beside Monto) after nightfall. Young girls and 'foul-mouthed soldiers startle the ears of passers-by with their horrifying cross-talk.'[2] Dublin Castle, the headquarters of the Dublin Metropolitan Police, was inundated with complaints from the public. Ross was forced to abandon his plan, advising that it would be for the best if the problem was confined to one part of the city rather than being dispersed all over it. Consequently, police raids on Monto ceased, business returned as normal and Dublin carried on as before, ignoring the problem. Lack of visibility and containment of the problem were the real issues for the authorities.[3]

The First World War brought an increase in business and Monto persevered for at least another ten years or so as a place of brothels, pubs, shebeens, crime and mayhem. However, the major blow to the area came when its financial viability became seriously undermined by the withdrawal of soldiers from the city following the War of Independence, Anglo-Irish Treaty (December 1921) and the establishment of the Irish Free State (6 December 1922). In December 1922 the Royal Barracks (now Collins) was the last to close and 5,000 troops marched down Dublin's Quays to the awaiting ships to bring them back to Britain.

This crucial factor, combined with a conservative spirit in the new Irish Free State (the greatest revolutionaries become the greatest conservatives), the determination of the Catholic Action group the Legion of Mary and its leader, Frank Duff, to close Monto, and the encouragement of Fr Richard Devane of the Jesuits, all combined to end the reign of the most notorious red-light district in Europe. But importantly, it was the loss of so many paying customers that made the job of the Legion of Mary much easier. The madams and the girls knew their business would be going into rapid decline with the departure of the thousands of soldiers that used to flock to Monto.[4]

British troops depart from Dublin's North Wall in December 1922. (Courtesy of Feeds Burner)

When the new energetic and progressive Chief Commissioner of the Dublin Metropolitan Police, General William Murphy (he was a military general, having served in the British Army during the First World War), drew up a report in 1925 on the problem in prostitution in the city; he noted that brothels in Monto operated essentially 'without much let or hindrance on the part of the police authorities'. This situation was finally confronted by State forces with a large-scale police raid on Monto for 12 March 1925.

FATHER DEVANE AND FRANK DUFF

But before we look at this final raid on Monto, we must consider the influence of Frank Duff and the lay Catholic organisation called the Legion of Mary. Duff has the honour of being the individual seen as being ultimately responsible for the eventual

Monto residents selling flowers outside Dublin's Pro-Cathedral in early twentieth century. Monto was just a few minutes away. (Courtesy of Fotofinish)

demise of Monto. A civil servant, he was one of the founders of the Legion of Mary. This was an offshoot of the St Vincent de Paul Society, at Myra House, Francis Street, in September 1921. He had been working with the poor of the Liberties, visiting houses, doing anti-proselytising work and trying to rescue girls from a life of prostitution. The latter he accidentally came across in the course of visiting lodging houses at no. 25 Chancery Lane, off Bride Street and across from St Patrick's Park and Cathedral. In the course of visiting the poor women dwellers of this house he discovered that most of them were in fact prostitutes, living there, but working in places like Monto.[5]

Between 1923 and 1925, Missions led by Frank Duff of the Legion of Mary, and Jesuit priest, Fr Richard Devane, worked to close down the brothels. The Legion was greatly encouraged by the Jesuits as well as local clergy based in Dublin's Pro-Cathedral, on Marlborough Street, only a stone's throw from the heart of Monto. The Jesuits, of course, would have been much scandalised by Monto, and particularly by the fact that one of their former pupils, James Joyce, who was educated at Belvedere College, Great Denmark Street, close to Monto, had written in a semi-autobiographical manner and very graphically about his experiences in the area in his *Portrait of the Artist as a Young Man* (1916). Their sensibilities would have been further rocked by the publication of *Ulysses* in 1922. Joyce's writing did not reflect well on the Jesuits. They would have been horrified that one of their boys should write such works as *Portrait* and *Ulysses*, which they would have regarded as pornographic, indecent and obscene. This precipitated the gathering and galvanising of Catholic forces in the new Irish Free State, to go on the attack once and for all that rid the city of Monto. Subsequently, Fr Richard Devane became the primary mover for censorship in Ireland in the 1920s, and his blueprint for it, encapsulated in a report presented to the new government in the mid-1920s, ultimately led to the Censorship of Publications Act 1929, with its emphasis on rooting out and banning 'obscene' literature.[6]

MAY OBLONG REJECTS DUFF'S ADVANCES

In the early 1920s, the Legion of Mary had managed to persuade some of the Monto prostitutes to abandon their old ways by offering alternative accommodation and material help and encouraging them to go on a religious retreat organised by the group. Duff decided to encourage others to follow suit by going directly into Monto. In his attempts to rescue some of the women from Monto, Duff was directed to May Oblong (the 'Queen of Monto') of no. 14 Corporation Street, who professed to have given up her business as a madam. Initially Oblong was helpful, and presented herself as a good-living Catholic, but when it was suggested that she could help the Legion remove the women from Monto, she angrily ejected Duff and an associate from her home. Duff saw racks of coats and hats on his way out 'and knew there was too much there for one woman'. May Oblong hadn't given up prostitution, but was a costumier for the prostitutes in Monto.

May Oblong and the rest of the madams eventually agreed to accept compensation of a few hundred pounds for having to close their businesses. They had initially sought £1,500 to cover their debts and losses. May Oblong, in the course of the negotiations, had threatened to open a brothel beside the Pro-Cathedral's parish priest's presbytery in nearby Marlborough Street if Duff did not agree to her demands.[7]

MIDNIGHT RAID ON MONTO

Devane and Duff also received the co-operation of Dublin Police Commissioner, General William Murphy, and their long campaign against Monto ended with 120 arrests and the closure of the brothels following a police raid.

Monto's closure was set for 12 March 1925 and, despite some Store Street officers who enjoyed the 'benefits' of Monto being

General W.R.E. Murphy, Training and Operations, Dublin Metropolitan Police, 1923. He was responsible for the raid on Monto on 12 March 1925. (Courtesy of Dublin Forums/ Damntheweather)

reluctant to close the brothels, a threat of dismissal from the Garda Commissioner to the local superintendent ensured Monto did indeed close on this date. The officers conducting the raid were under the command of David Neligan, Chief Superintendent of the Detective Branch, and Captain Ennis, Assistant Superintendent. On 12 March 1925, at the instigation of the Legion, in a midnight raid, police cars swooped on the area, emptying the brothels of clients and madams and into the police vans. The 120 people arrested included a Dáil deputy, who insisted he was 'only there for a drink', and other well-known dignitaries.

The event was in the newspapers the next morning with headlines such as 'Mystery Raid on City's Black Spot'. The *Irish Independent* reported that 'quite a sensation was created' with the 'sudden descent upon the area' and noted that it was part of a campaign that had been going on for some time 'for clearing certain areas of frequenters of disorderly houses'. It noted that

'Dublin police, as a result of a midnight swoop on a congested district in the northern area, last night made 120 arrests, those arrested being mostly young men and women.' The *Cork Examiner*, under the heading 'Darkest Dublin', advised its readers that 'no citizen of Dublin will need to be told why a wholesale raid was carried out in the early hours of this morning in the network of streets lying between Marlborough Street and Amiens Street'. It stated that Monto was 'where all law is scorned', and contained 'a large number of persons who have every reason to be afraid of the police'. It described Monto as a 'plague spot, where criminals could safely lurk' and stated that 'robbers and shebeen owners can abide there safely'. It reported that all this was shattered by the raid. However, of these arrests, only two would be charged, with one, Polly Butler, receiving a six-week sentence; this was the only jail term ever given to a madam in the area's history.[8]

The raid was followed by members of the Legion marching into Monto, past the remaining kneeling prostitutes, blessing each brothel and pinning a religious picture to each door. Frank Duff went to the back of Corporation Buildings (formerly Mabbot Street) and proceeded to hang a huge crucifix to the wall, sending a clear message that the days of Monto were well and truly over. Many of the remaining prostitutes moved into hostels, including the Sancta Maria on Harcourt Street, run by the Legion of Mary. This building had been former premises for the Sinn Féin party and was frequently used by Michael Collins. It was given to the Legion by William T. Cosgrave, head of Irish Free State's Cumann na nGaedhael government.

Duff estimated that there were 200 girls working in Monto in 1922. The number had been reduced to forty by 1925. Some of those who remained working the streets, however, became victims of the desire to deal with prostitution by hiding the prostitutes and then ignoring them, including those who ended up in the Magdalen laundries (like the one in Gloucester Street) where a distinction was made between those 'first fallen' and 'habitual offenders'. It was telling that prostitutes who were convicted in the courts often expressed a preference to go to Mountjoy for six months rather than a Magdalen Laundry, where the incarceration could be much longer and, in some cases, indefinite.

Contrary to the widespread belief, the Legion of Mary did not get rid of the problem. It just dispersed it further afield. Some of the prostitutes took whatever alternative was available – Legion of Mary hostels, Magdalen Laundries or the boat to England to pursue their careers there. But many remained in Dublin and continued trading in the Stephen's Green area (near the Shelbourne Hotel) and elsewhere. Most significantly, the underlying social problems of unemployment and appalling living conditions in tenements did not go away. The fledgling Irish Free State could do little to tackle these economic problems and the powerful and influential Catholic Church, in very unambiguous language, told the Legion of Mary, the Catholic Truth Society of Ireland and the broader Catholic Action Movement in the 1920s and 1930s, to stay well clear of the

Plaque on house in Dublin's Francis Street, in the Liberties, where Frank Duff's organisation, the Legion of Mary, was founded in 1921.

A May Procession coming into St Mary's Mansions from Railway Street, 1960s.
To the front of the photo, surrounded by the Gardai, are some of the women from
the Gloucester Street Magdalen Laundry. (Courtesy of Dublin Forums/Rashers)

'social question', as these problems were called, and not to bring
it to public attention at any of their conferences or congresses.
Instead the many Catholic lay organisations were to focus their
energies on censorship and moral issues.

Consequently, the post-revolutionary conservative energies
of the Irish Free State went into overdrive in the 1920s to
impose censorship on anything deemed indecent or obscene.
In 1923, strict censorship in film was introduced and films
'indecent, obscene or blasphemous or contrary to, or subver-
sive of public morality' were banned. 1924 saw the restrictions
placed on the sale of alcohol not least as it was seen as one of the
causes of slipping morality. By 1929, and following a long and
protracted campaign, with Fr Richard Devane in its vanguard,
the Censorship of Publications Act enabled the government to

ban 'indecent and obscene' books and reading material, ushering in an era of draconian censorship that stifled much creativity and that lasted more than forty years.[9]

Conditions are much different now. Montgomery Street has become Foley Street, and Mecklenburgh Street and Tyrone Street are now Railway Street. Today most of Monto has vanished into offices, apartments and Dublin Corporation/Dublin City Council housing developments such as Liberty House. However, some names linger from the past; Mabbot Lane, running from Talbot Street to Railway Street, Bella Street, Beaver Row, and John Mullet's pub (est. 1893) survive as reminders of a different era and a unique area.[10]

MONTO IN REVOLUTIONARY TIMES

THE 1913 LOCKOUT

The Monto area of Dublin featured in some of Dublin's and Ireland's major historical dramas in the early twentieth century. During one of Dublin's most turbulent political periods, the 1913 Dublin Lockout, Gardiner Street and other parts of Monto played a key role. This may be seen from the *Report of the Dublin Disturbances Commission* of 1914 and is not surprising, since many of the workers having to bear the brunt of very demanding and difficult working conditions lived there, whether they be dockers, railway workers, tram drivers or casual labourers.

Poverty, low wages, casual work, strikes, discrimination etc. impacted on this area more than any other place in Dublin and thus places such as Gardiner Street and Foley Street hosted numerous meetings of those involved in the strike and Lockout, including those organised by Labour and trade union leader James Larkin. Such was the heightened tension and the deplorable working and living conditions of those from Monto, that in order to show solidarity, both Maud Gonne and Countess Constance Markeivicz visited the area at the time of the Lockout. Furthermore, many of those arrested during the street riots in Sackville Street were

Barefooted tenement children
from Monto area in 1913.
(Courtesy of GCI/harvest)

Tenement girls from Monto collecting firewood after the 1916 Rising.
(Courtesy of Dublin Forums/Damntheweather)

from Foley Street, Buckingham Street, Gloucester Street and Corporation Street.

Foley Street was the scene of much serious fighting on 30 August 1913, during the early days of the Dublin Lockout. A police raid on protesters' homes saw several houses destroyed and two activists, James Nolan and John Byrne, killed, following serious injuries. In fact, this brutal attack on the workers generated much reaction and heightened the tensions of downtrodden workers, and it sparked the real beginning of the General Lockout of the workers of Dublin in 1913.

According to one section of an official report:

Gloucester Street, Waterford Street, Gardiner Street, and Parnell Street, 31 August 1913:

About 5 p.m. on Sunday evening, the 31st August, extensive rioting prevailed in the district around Gardiner Street, and crowds assembled in that street, and at the corners of streets communicating therewith. In the first instance the police came into contact with the rioters at the corner of Gloucester Street, and dispersed them after being met with a fusillade of stones and bricks, in many cases thrown from houses. A number of troopers were engaged in keeping the crowd moving, but their efforts were greatly hampered by the persistent stone throwing that took place from nearly all the houses in the streets through which they passed. In some of the streets, notably Cumberland Street and Waterford Street, numbers of men were stationed on the roofs of houses, and stripped off slates and tiles for the purpose of throwing them into the street at passing constables. In one case in Waterford Street seven men were discovered on the roof of a house. This disturbance was spread over the entire district, and the serious feature of it was the readiness of the occupants of the various tenement houses to shelter escaping rioters, and to join with them in attacking the police from the upper stories of many houses. Some baton charges were made, but as a rule these were useless, as the crowds fled before the police and took refuge in houses which were open to receive them.[1]

Dublin's Sackville Street with Nelson's Pillar in background, *c.* 1900. (Courtesy of GCI/harvest)

'No room in the tenements', homeless children in Monto area, early 1900s. Notice one of the children has no shoes, a regular feature in Dublin until the famous Herald Boot Fund of the 1940s. (Courtesy of GCI)

Monto residents were some of the people hardest hit and downtrodden by years of unrelenting apathy and might of most employers. Consequently, Monto residents played a huge part in the movement to strike a blow for workers' rights in Dublin. Following the Lockout, employers had to have a different view of their employees, and it marked the beginning of an improvement in workers' rights and conditions of labour.

THE 1916 RISING

Monto also played a very important role in the 1916 Rising and the War of Independence. A number of streets in Monto are historically very significant in the fight for Irish independence. And many of the Volunteers who fought and died for Irish Independence came from Monto. Moreover, many of the workers of Monto were not only members, but formed the very backbone of James Connolly's Irish Citizens Army. Residents of Monto were more inclined to join with James Connolly rather than the Irish Volunteers.

One of the leaders of 1916 was born in the tenements of Monto. Seán Heuston (1891-1916) was born at 24 Lower Gloucester Street, Dublin, the son of John Heuston, a clerk, and Maria McDonald, an envelope maker. He was educated to intermediate grade by the Christian Brothers at O'Connell's Schools on North Richmond Street, not too far from where he lived. During the 1916 Rising, he commanded the Mendicity Institute, an important post overlooking the River Liffey. From here he was able to influence the movement of the Crown Forces based at the Royal (Collins) Barracks trying to approach the city and the Four Courts. He was the youngest of those executed in 1916.

As well as being the location for some of the planning of the revolution, some of the Monto prostitutes did some important work on behalf of the revolutionaries. The ladies, besides loosening the belts of some of their soldier customers, loosened their tongues for useful information and also relieved them of some of

1917 image of Peadar Kearney who penned the National Anthem, 'The Soldier's Song', and whose sister Kathleen was the mother of Irish writer Brendan Behan. He named his son Pearse.(Courtesy of Dublin Forums/Damntheweather)

their arms and munitions. They helped the revolutionary effort by passing on soldiers' idle talk and pillow secrets, as well as the armaments.

Four of the thirty-eight children killed during the 1916 Rising were from Monto: Christina Caffrey (age 2) from no. 27 Corporation Buildings; Charles Darcy (age 15) from no. 4 Murphy's Cottages, Gloucester Street; Patrick Ivors (age 14) from no. 15 Cumberland Street; and Patrick Kelly (age 12) from no. 24 Buckingham Buildings.

Molly O'Reilly lived on Gardiner Street. In 1916 the 14-year-old girl had the honour of hoisting the green flag of the Irish Citizen Army over Liberty Hall (the old Liberty Hall) on Palm Sunday at the request of James Connolly. On that day he presented her with the flag which she brought to the parapet of the building and with the help of a chair, she reached the rope and raised the flag. As a strong supporter of the cause of Irish freedom, she also acted as a despatch courier between City Hall and the GPO on Easter Monday.

At the corner of Railway Street and Lower Gardiner Street there is a plaque on the wall commemorating Patrick Heeny (1881–1911), who had lived at no. 101 Railway Street. In 1907 the music to Ireland's national anthem ('Amhran na bhFiann',

Barefooted Monto children, 1912. (Courtesy of GCI/harvest)

'Soldier's Song') was composed by Heeney at his home at what was then no. 101 Mecklenburg Street. His fellow Irish patriot, Peadar Kearney, wrote the song's lyrics, also in 1907, and assisted Heeney with the music. Patrick Heeney never lived to see his music become famous; he died in abject poverty in 1911 aged 29. The song became the battle hymn of the republic for the men and women of the 1916 Rising and was later sung in the various internment camps and prisons, following the Rising.[2]

THE WAR OF INDEPENDENCE AND SHANAHAN'S PUB

Monto was also a hive of IRA activity, particularly around the time of the War of Independence, with several safe houses for the Michael Collins' flying columns. During the Black and Tan years of 1920 and 1921 many activists with the Dublin Brigade of the IRA hid out in Monto for safety, knowing full well that such was the area's reputation that even the Dublin Metropolitan Police dared not enter after dark. Very importantly, not only had the area had several safe-houses but local paperboys acted as intelligence sources, keeping tabs on the movements of those in Dublin Castle.

Two Monto pubs featured prominently in the War of Independence: Phil Shanahan's, grocer and publican at 134 Foley Street, and Thomas Hynes, tea, wine and spirit merchant at no. 19 Lower Gloucester Place – at the junction of Gloucester Place and Lower Gloucester Street (now Lower Sean McDermott Street).

Phil Shanahan was originally from Tipperary and was a member of the Irish Republican Army. He saw action in Boland's Mills with Eamon De Valera at the time of the Easter Rising in 1916. He was a licensed vintner and because of his involvement in the Easter Rising, he subsequently had difficulties over the renewal of the licence for his public house. Shanahan consulted the lawyer and politician Timothy Healy who was able to get the licence renewed. Healy described Shanahan as jolly and

"All I ask of you is, that wherever you may be, you will remember me at the Altar of the Lord."

May the Sacred Heart of Jesus be everywhere known and loved. —300 days' Indulgence.

Jesus, meek and humble of Heart, make my heart like unto Thine. —300 days' Indulgence.

In Ever Loving Memory
—OF—
SEAUN ALLIS TREACY,
SOLOHEADBEG, CO. TIPPERARY,

COMMANDANT I.R.A.,

Killed in action in Talbot Street, Dublin,

On October 13th, 1920,

whilst fighting for Irish Freedom.

AGED 24 YEARS.

R. I. P.

Make me a grave where the shamrocks grow,
Say that I fell fighting the foe;
Fought best I could, gave blow for blow,
And died for our dear Mother Erin.

In memoriam card for Sean Treacy, killed in action in Talbot Street, during the War of Independence. (Courtesy of GCI/harvest)

The girl in the right of the photo is Linda Kearns, a trained nurse from Sligo who took part in the Easter Rising. She ran a nursing home in Gardiner Place, off Gardiner Street, which was used as a safe house for men on the run from the British military. She avoided arrest after the rising. During the War of Independence she did intelligence work for the IRA and carried messages and explosives. (Courtesy of Dublin Forums/Rashers)

respectable. He was a Tipperary hurler in the old days. Shanahan was elected an MP in 1918 and was arrested and detained in custody by the authorities in April 1920 but was released in time to attend the next meeting of the Dáil on 29 June 1920. His premises in Dublin were a safe haven for many in the IRA from outside Dublin, including Sean Treacy, Dan Breen and Sean Hogan, while they attended meetings in Dublin. The doctor,

Group of Black and Tans in central Dublin during the War of Independence, 1921. (Courtesy of GCI)

writer and former fellow student of James Joyce, Oliver St John Gogarty recalled being at Shanahan's in Foley Street: 'The prostitutes used to pinch the guns and ammunition from the Auxiliaries and Black and Tans at night and then leave them for us at Phil Shanahan's public house.' He also said that 'Shanahan's was the rendezvous of saints and sinners'. Upstairs in Shanahan's there was a room that was a regular rendezvous for Michael Collins and local IRA commanders including Sean Treacy and Dan Breen. Furthermore, arms and munitions were often stored in the premises.[3] In 2014 a commemorative plaque was erected on a wall where the pub originally stood.

HYNES PUB AND DUBLIN CASTLE

On 5 February 1921 Lance Corporal John Ryan was murdered in a pub in Monto. It was believed that Ryan was spying on wanted men hiding out in Monto. An IRA hit squad of Bill Stapleton, Eddie Byrnes and Paddy Kennedy walked into Hynes Pub on the corner of Old Gloucester Place and Lower Gloucester Street and shot Ryan dead. Ryan had entered the pub with his brother-in-law, the husband of infamous Monto madam Becky Cooper. Michael Collins believed that IRA leaders Brigadier Dick McKee and Vice-Brigadier Peadar Clancy were betrayed to Crown forces by Ryan. McKee and Clancy had been captured at Sean Fitzpatrick's house at 36 Gloucester Street by the army and Black and Tans in

Scene in the Monto area after War of Independence. (Courtesy of GCI)

IN MEMORY OF
VICE BRIGADIER
SEAN TRACEY,
3RD (SOUTH) TIPPERARY BRIGADE
I.R.A.
KILLED IN ACTION BY BRITISH
FORCES OUTSIDE THIS
HOUSE 14TH OCTOBER 1920.
Go nDéinidh Día
Trócaire Air.
ERECTED BY NATIONAL
GRAVES ASSOCIATION.
1937.

Plaque on Talbot Street wall to commemorate War of Independence leader Sean Tracey (also known as Sean Treacy). (Courtesy of Irish Volunteers)

the early hours of 21 November 1920. Both men were brought to the Guard Room of Dublin Castle, and the next day tortured and murdered along with Irish Volunteer Conor Clune. This was in reprisal after IRA units smashed the elite spy network of British Intelligence the previous day.

Dan Breen, in his book on his fight for Irish freedom, noted that Ryan had telephoned the information on McKee and Clancy to Dublin Castle and the house at Gloucester Street was then raided by the Tans in the early hours of the morning. The details of the phone call must have been transmitted back to the IRA from one of its Dublin Castle insiders. According to Dan Breen, 'known as Shankers Ryan, he was a brother of Becky Cooper, a brothel keeper. He was executed for his treachery. For some time prior to Bloody Sunday (when soldiers opened fire on the crowd in Croke Park killing many) we had suspected him of spying.'[4]

Today, there are two plaques on Sean McDermott Street commemorating the patriots who gave their lives for Irish freedom. The first, at no. 36, commemorates McKee and Clancy. Further down the street on the opposite side, Captain Sean Connolly is commemorated outside no. 58 where he had lived. Connolly was killed in action on Easter Monday 1916 on the roof of City Hall by a British Army sniper. His four brothers and sister also fought for Irish freedom in Easter Week.

Other streets and individuals in Monto also figured prominently in 1916 and the War of Independence. Amiens Street was

Plaque at the junction of Gardiner Street and Great Denmark Street commemorating those who fought in the Irish War of Independence from the Monto area.

where 1916 leader Tom Clarke had his tobacconist shop for many years; first it was located at no. 55 and later at no 77. Nearby is the North Star Hotel, the venue of a meeting between Padraig Pearse and Michael Colivet of the Limerick Brigade, just a few days before the 1916 Rising, to discuss and confirm plans. Phil Sheerin's Coolevin Dairy was located under the railway bridge and it was an important intelligence and weapons depot for Michael Collins.

J. & M. Cleary's pub is unique for a number of reasons. Formerly known as the Signal House, it is located under the railway bridge and across from Connolly Station. It has been in the same family since the mid-1800s, and being staunch Republicans during the War of Independence the bar was a meeting place for famous Irish Republicans such as Michael Collins. Images of him adorn many of the walls inside. In fact, some scenes of the film on Collins' life were shot in here for that very reason. There are very few other places in Dublin, save perhaps the Long Hall, that have retained so much of their original appearance. There are also old images of Monto and the madam, Becky Cooper, adorning the walls.

Number 41 Gardiner Street Upper was the home of Joe McGuinness, elected as a Sinn Féin TD for Longford South to the first Dáil in 1918 while in Lewes Gaol, under the slogan of 'Vote him in to get him out'. During the Easter Rising in 1916 McGuinness was involved in commandeering the Four Courts for the Volunteers. Kevin O'Higgins also lived on Gardiner Street for a while, going under the name of Mr Wilson. No. 14 Gardiner Street Lower was home to Sean O'Reilly, a 1916 Volunteer who was killed in action in City Hall on 24 April 1916. A few doors away the famous Moran's Hotel is at no.17 at the junction with Talbot Street. Countess Markievicz was a sniper here during the Civil War and Cumann na mBan was also based here during hostilities. No. 35 Gardiner Street Lower was the Typographical Union Hall, the head office of the very strong Dublin Printer's Union. This was a very important meeting place for IRB members and the Dublin Brigade, as many union

British Army checkpoint at the corner of Summerhill and Gardiner Street, 1916. (Courtesy of GCI)

members were Volunteers and fought in the War of Independence. Michael Collins used this building to meet and plan very important activities.

Around the corner in Gloucester Street (Sean McDermott Street) another printer's union had its headquarters. The Tara Hall Printer's Union was the meeting place for the C Company, 2nd Battalion, of the IRB Dublin Brigade, under the command of Dick McKee. No. 15 Gloucester Street was the Painter's Hall and where C Company, 3rd Battalion met. No. 35 Gloucester Street was home to long-time trade union leader Tom MacPartlin and above him the offices of the Builder's and Carpenter's Union. Next door, no. 36, was used as a 'safe house' and unfortunately Dick McKee and Peadar Clancy were arrested there on the night of 20–21 November 1920.

Monto was also the home of the patriot Frank Flood who lived at 30 Summerhill Parade. On 14 March 1921 he was executed for his involvement in the War of Independence. He was a brilliant engineering student in his second year at the National University of Ireland. He was a first Lieutenant Dublin Brigade IRA. Frank was also a member of the fifty-strong Dublin ASU, set up in December to implement the GHQ directive to increase the IRA offensive. The best Volunteers from the battalions were selected and combined to create a more effective operational structure against Crown Forces. He was among the Volunteers who took part in the raid on the King's Inn armoury in Dublin and was also involved in the many attempts to help Kevin Barry escape.

Flood was also the leader of the abortive 'Drumcondra Ambush' when a proposed attack on a Dublin Metropolitan Police tender

Undercover men provided information to the British on the activities of the Irish Republican Army during the War of Independence. Many of the Cairo Gang were assassinated by Michael Collins's men on 21 November 1920. There is no known photograph of this gang, so the group in this photo is probably the Igoe Gang (sometimes known as the 'Murder Gang'). These were RIC men and collaborators who were brought to Dublin to identify and target IRA men from their respective counties outside the capital. (Courtesy of Irish Volunteers)

was thwarted due to the actions of an informer. Frank was captured while attempting to escape the scene. He was found guilty of high treason and was hanged in Mountjoy Jail at the age of 19. He was the only student, other than Kevin Barry, to be executed and his execution gave rise to large demonstrations and protests. Prior to his execution, he wrote in a letter to his brother Alfie 'there must be no weeping for me. I am going where I might never have reached if I had lived my ordinary life'. When his father said to him that efforts for a reprieve were being made, Frank said: 'We ask not for a reprieve, but for justice'.

No. 39 Mabbot Street was the birthplace of William Rooney. He was a friend and advisor of the founder of Sinn Féin, Arthur Griffith, and was very much involved in the Celtic Revival. He did much to promote the Irish language also. He was involved in the founding of the Celtic Literary Society and was a frequent contributor to Griffith's *United Irishman* newspaper.

Frank Flood lived at 30 Summerhill Parade in Dublin's north inner city. He was a brilliant engineering student in his second year at UCD. He was a first lieutenant, ASU Dublin Brigade IRA. He was also the leader of the abortive 'Drumcondra Ambush'. Frank was captured while attempting to escape the scene. (Courtesy of GCI/harvest)

In the heart of Monto: children in Rutland Street School in the 1930s. (Courtesy of GCI)

Talbot Street, on the edge of Monto, was also the location for much action. Seán Treacy (1895–1920) was one of the leaders of the 3rd Tipperary Brigade of the Irish Republican Army during the War of Independence. He was killed in October 1920, in Talbot Street in a shoot-out with soldiers during an aborted British Secret Service surveillance operation.

Monto was also a hive of IRA activity during the subsequent Civil War, where again many Irregulars, who opposed the Anglo-Irish Treaty that ended the War of Independence, found food and shelter there. Unfortunately, so too were many volunteers on the opposing side and consequently there was much violence in the area.[5]

DICEY, ROSIE AND KITTY: MONTO IN SONG AND STORY

Such was the infamy and notoriety surrounding Monto, with more than a hint of danger and adventure, that it has captured the imagination of songwriters, balladeers, and the literati. There is an old Dublin street song that used to be sung by children as a skipping rhyme, about Mabbot Lane and prostitution:

> Down in Mabbot Lane
> Lives a big fat lady
> If you want to know her name
> You have to pay a shilling
> Soldiers two and six
> Sailors two a penny
> Big fat men two pound ten
> Little kids a penny.

The medical surgeon and writer (and also friend of James Joyce) Oliver St John Gogarty, wrote a tribute to Joyce and his visits to Monto:

> There is a young fellow named Joyce,
> Who possesses a sweet tenor voice.
> He goes down to the Kips,

With a psalm on his lips,
And biddeth the harlots rejoice.[1]

(Reproduced by kind permission of Ulick O'Connor)

Gogarty also wrote a ballad commemorating the Hay Hotel in Parnell Street, not far from Monto, and in it he remembers his youth in Monto:

Where are the great Kip Bullies gone?
The bookies and the outrageous whores
Whom we gladly rode upon
When youth was mine and youth was yours;
Tyrone Street of the crowded doors,
And Faithful Place so infidel.

(Reproduced by kind permission of Ulick O'Connor)

Having a chat outside a
tenement dwelling on Sean
McDermott Street
in the 1940s.
(Courtesy of
Dublin Forums)

Some of the famous madams appear in the Dublin street ballad *Dicey Reilly*. One of the verses goes:

> Long years ago when men were men and fancied May Oblong
> Or lovely Becky Cooper or Maggie's Mary Wong
> One woman put them all to shame, just one was worthy of the name,
> And the name of that dame was Dicey Reilly. (Anonymous)

TAKE HER UP TO MONTO

There is also a Dublin ballad, *Monto (Take Her Up to Monto)*, written by George Desmond Hodnett former music critic of *The Irish Times* and popularised by the famous The Dubliners folk and ballad group.

The next line is usually a rude line or noise added in by the singer or the audience, such as: 'Balls to you!'

However, although written in 1958, it was not until Ronnie Drew of The Dubliners included it in the groups programme at the Gate Theatre in 1966, that it became widely known. After his unique rendition of it in his inimitable deep Dublin gravelly voice, the ballad became an instant hit.[2]

Sailors in Kingstown (Dún Laoghaire) in 1900.
(Courtesy of Dublin Forums)

226

Monto is also twice mentioned in the Irish folk song 'Waxies' Dargle': 'I went up to Monto Town, to see Uncle McCardle ...' And: 'If we went up to Monto Town, we might get a drink for nuttin' ...'

THE WHOREMASTER AND THE WHOREMISTRESS: JAMES JOYCE'S MONTO

In the area of literature and folklore, Monto has also fuelled the imagination of many. As a student, the writer James Joyce was a frequent visitor to Monto and the experience inspired some of his greatest writings, including *Portrait of the Artist as a Young Man* (1916) and *Ulysses* (1922). The area was immortalised as 'Nighttown' (originally referred to the night shift of newspaper staff) in the 'Circe' chapter of Joyce's most famous work, *Ulysses*, where the central figures Leopold Bloom and Stephen Dedalus visit a brothel in Monto.[3]

From an early age Joyce was obsessed by the mysteries of sexuality, sexual frustration and illicit satisfaction. While he was a secondary school student at Belvedere College, where he was enrolled from 1893 until he turned 16 five years later, he had his first sexual experience at the age of 14 – with a Dublin prostitute; Belvedere of course, being only a stone's throw from the very heart of Monto. It has been said that it was in Monto that he learned how to have sexual intercourse, although there is no independent witness to the fact. However, his *Portrait of the Artist as a Young Man* appears to be semi-autobiographical and the main character Stephen Dedalus has his visits to Monto very vividly depicted by Joyce. Moreover, in colourful language, Joyce in *Ulysses* captures the old bawd's cries outside a brothel in Monto: 'maidenhead inside ....you won't get a virgin in the flash houses'. [4]

Appalling as it may sound today, Joyce was of his time; sexual initiation was with prostitutes – this was regard as de rigueur for young men. If he did go to Monto then presumably he did not go there just for the drink or just to observe. For years he prowled the streets of the area. There he encountered the world of pimps and prostitutes, the sounds of drunken revelry, and witnessed life's underbelly. Consequent to these early visits to Monto he experienced guilt, went to Confession and tried to reform. But Monto won in the end. It was hugely significant for Joyce that the ensnaring power of urgent desire, raw lust and sex, and the themes of sin and guilt, gave potent force and originality to his writings.

Years later, in 1909, Joyce returned home from self-imposed exile in Paris, and visited Monto again. This time he was with his friend from his Trinity College Dublin days, Vincent Cosgrove. He spent nights drinking and whoring, visiting his old haunts and brothels in the area. Likewise when his mother died, he returned home and revisited the brothels with his friends Oliver St John Gogarty and Cosgrove. There he found plenty

A young James Joyce. He was a regular visitor to Monto in his student days and the area was pivotal in the inspiration for *Ulysses* and *Portrait of the Artist as a Young Man* and other writings. (Courtesy of GCI/harvest)

of sex but not love. And he also acquired gonorrhoea, according to some Joycean experts. Richard Ellmann, the foremost Joyce biographer, however, never suggested he suffered from the disease. However, to this day, experts are reluctant to agree that the author's poor eyesight and possibly early death was the result of venereal disease. More recent commentators and biographers are questioning why was he taking arsenic – was it to help cure syphilis? But it is agreed by many scholars that he frequented the brothels of Monto in his youth and that he was promiscuous.

Commentators on Joyce say he was a voyeur and a troubled genius and one having had a hedonistic lifestyle thanks to Monto. His idea of women was a very troubled one – he had this idea of them either as mothers or whores in that the women were either for pro-creation purposes to create and sustain a family; or were for 'real' sex, gratification, pleasure, desire – as with prostitutes. In his own personal life and during the course of his relationship and marriage to Nora Barnacle, it was well-known that he was unfaithful to the one great love of his life.

This obsession with the female form is manifest in *Portrait of the Artist as a Young Man* and the 'Circe' chapter of *Ulysses*. In these books he vividly describes the seedy brothels of Monto, the squalid streets and lanes, the depraved sexual obscenities, the lively pubs and the endless amount of foul language. He was enticed by the strange, the beautiful, the bliss, the horror, the squalor, the macabre and the magic of Monto, as he perceived it. Stephen Dedalus' experiences and sexual liaisons with prostitutes as he makes his way through the shadowy and gas-lit streets and alleys of Monto are well depicted. The prostitutes are described as 'pox-fouled wenches of the taverns'.[7] Two of the prostitutes portrayed by Joyce, Florry Talbot and Kitty Ricketts, were based on Monto prostitute Fleury Crawford and brothel madam Becky Cooper.

Here in Monto Joyce describes how some of the prostitutes were attired and behaved:

Cheap whores, singly, coupled, shawled, dishevelled, call from lanes, doorways, corners. 'Are you going far, queer fellow? How's your middle leg? Got a match on you? Eh, come here till I stiffen it for you.' Or, 'Coming in to have a short time.' And, 'Hello Bertie, any good on your mind.[8]

Even before it was published in 1922, James Joyce's *Ulysses* was already causing ructions. The chapter dealing with Monto was part of the problem. Already in April 1921, the husband of one of the several typists who was engaged to prepare the 'Circe' (Monto) episode read Joyce's manuscript and threw a portion of it in the fire. *Ulysses* was not banned in Ireland, but was not imported, for fear of prosecution. Even some of Joyce's literary contemporaries expressed disapproval of the novel. D.H. Lawrence regarded Molly Bloom's soliloquy at the end of the novel as 'the dirtiest, most indecent, obscene thing ever written' and told his wife: 'This *Ulysses* muck is more disgusting than Casanova.' Virginia Woolf was shocked by the 'obscenity' she encountered in *Ulysses*.

Ulysses was like a bomb going off in the prison of English literature. Everything was fair game to him. In the chapter with the brothel scene, he gives the reader a shocking portrayal of Monto. But that, seemingly, was part of his artistic programme. What shocked people about *Ulysses* is the focus on the practices of sexuality – the sheer nature of desire and lust that men and women can feel. No publisher in Ireland would touch *Ulysses* when Joyce had finished the work. It was fortunate for him that Sylvia Beach, the owner of the Shakespeare Book Company in Paris, published a limited edition for him. The book produced unprecedented outrage and disgust when published in 1922. In the USA and Britain, to possess a copy of the book was a criminal offence. Many thought the work obscene. But Joyce's view was that if *Ulysses* was not fit to read, then life was not fit to live because there was nothing in the book that was not occurring every day in Dublin. But it caused scandal in Ireland

and throughout the world for the open sexuality that the book expressed.[9]

Most of the action of the controversial 'Circe' chapter takes place in the disorderly house of Bella Cohen in Mecklenburgh Street. Mrs Cohen is described as 'a massive whoremistress, dressed in a three-quarter ivory gown, fringed round the hem with tasselled selvedge, and cools herself, flirting a black horn fan like Minnie Hauch in *Carmen*. Her eyes are deeply carboned ... olive face is heavy. Her falcon eyes glitter...' And Joyce's description of Kitty Ricketts as 'a bony pallid whore ...' is a reminder of the renowned madam Becky Cooper when she was a young prostitute in the early years of the twentieth century.[10]

On their way home from Monto to the Cabmen's Shelter at the nearby Customs House, Leopold Bloom and Stephen Dedalus in *Ulysses* pass Dan Bergin's Pub (now Lloyds) at the corner of Amiens and Foley Streets. They continue their journey past Mullets pub which is still there (est. 1893) beside Lloyds, and also past the Signal House (now J. & M. Cleary's), the backdoor of the Dublin City Morgue at nos 2–4 Amiens Street with the main entrance on Store Street) and on towards the Dock Tavern pub (still there under a different name) on the corner of Amiens and Store Streets.

A few doors away from Cleary's is the North Star Hotel, a landmark Georgian period hotel steeped in history and with a notable mention as Bloom and Dedalus make their difficult and drunken journey homeward from Monto.

TUMBLING IN THE HAY WITH GOGARTY, BECKET AND BEHAN

Joyce's friend, fellow-student, and later medical doctor and Senator in the newly-independent Ireland in the 1920s, Oliver St John Gogarty, too had some first-hand experience of Monto and wrote about it in two of his most famous books – *Tumbling in the Hay* and *As I Walk Down Sackville Street*. Gogarty nicknamed Joyce 'the virginal kip-ranger'.

Tumbling in the Hay recounts one incident in a cheap brothel when the customer meets Mrs Mack, the madam who says to him: 'Lookit that! There ye are now, the ballroom's empty and all the bitches gone to bed.' And referring to the drunken pianist in the room, she continues, 'Look at it now. There's Lar in an empty room, playin' paralytic to a pint.'[11]

Gogarty also wrote a ballad about a local hotel called the decline of the popular Hay Hotel near Monto:

There's nothing left but ruin now
Where once the crazy cabfuls roared;
Where new-come sailors turned the prow
And love-locked cattle-dealers snored:
The room where old Luke Irwin whored,
The stairs on which John Elwood fell...

Where is Piano Mary, say?
Who dwelt where Hell's Gates leave the street,
And all the tunes she used to play
Along your spine beneath the sheet?
She was a morsel passing sweet
And warmer than the gates of hell.
Who tunes her now between the feet?
Go ask them at the Hay Hotel.[12]

(Reproduced by kind permission of Ulick O'Connor)

According to Gogarty, medical students were immune from molestation even in the most lawless part of town – Monto. Recalling his time as a medical student in Dublin he quotes an all-knowing cute local resident from Monto observing some such students visiting the area: 'Mebbe they're on midwifery duty, helping a poor woman. Ye never know.' Gogarty said they were:

Safe in every shebeen from the Gloucester Diamond to Hell's Gates when the 'kips' were in full blast. This side of the Yoshiwara there was never such as street as Tyrone Street for squalor with wildest orgies mixed. Here reigned the Shakespearean London of Jack Greene. Here nothing but the English language was undefiled. The names of its brothel-keepers, bullies, and frequenters were typical of a city which, like Vienna, had forged for itself a distinct identity. There were certainly neither Irish nor wholly English names. Dublin names, euphonious and romantic![13]

THE INFORMER IN MONTO

Liam O'Flaherty's very dark and atmospheric book, *The Informer*, touching on the War of Independence, and published in the mid-1920s, also brings us into the shadowy and bawdy world of Monto. Gypo Nolan, the main character, having been paid handsomely by Dublin Castle for information about a comrade-in-arms, suddenly realises in a Judas-like moment the enormity and horror of the betrayal, and flees to the safety of Monto. Here he is drawn to the strains of music and the snatches of distant song. He passes the 'long, low street of brothels, entwined like web-work among the ruins of what was a resort of the nobility in eighteenth-century Dublin...' Nolan wanted to get lost here, 'to go among beautiful women ... He wanted to go mad ... It was a mad night ...' He ended up in a brothel with laughter and drunken singing. The heat and atmosphere, with perfume and alcohol making for a heady cocktail, in the brothel overwhelmed and drew him in. He noticed the walls draped with pictures of women in amorous poses. The brothel was crowded with a party who had hired the premises for the night and who were there for a good time. There were ten prostitutes present also. Once Nolan showed his money, and called for 'drinks on the house', he was welcomed and quickly the orgy began. He soon struck up with a prostitute called Connemara Maggie, who 'enveloped his neck with her brawny arms'.[14]

BECKETT AND BEHAN

Samuel Becket's novel *Mercier and Camier* is known to refer to one of the madams – Becky Cooper. In the novel frequent visits are paid to 'Helen's Place', a bawdy house modelled on that of legendary Dublin madam Becky Cooper (and much like Becky Cooper, Helen has a talking parrot). Madams such as Becky Cooper and May Oblong are mentioned in Roddy Doyle's book *A Star Called Henry*.

Brendan Behan was born in a Russell Street tenement within earshot of Monto. His uncle was Peadar Kearney, who wrote the Irish National Anthem. Brendan's family lived in a room in a tenement and on the other side of the dividing wall he could hear the sounds of the prostitutes and their customers performing their tricks, as he later recalled. These experiences had a lasting influence on him. In the course of Behan's *The Quare Fellow* three old prisoners in Mountjoy Jail reminisce on Monto in the old days and madams and ladies of Monto such as Meena La Bloom and May Oblong. One of the prisoners recalls 'one night in the Digs' when he helped May relieve a Member of Parliament of his trousers. The MP 'who was going over the North Wall that morning to vote for Home Rule' was locked in a back room while May rifled his pockets looking for money. 'For the love of your country and mine', he shouted under the door to May, 'give me back me trousers'. 'So I will', says May, 'if you shove a fiver out under the door.'

Another prisoner (with a great imagination!) recounted the time when May Oblong was arrested during the War of Independence for breaking curfew. According to the prisoner, she was fined for having concealed about her person two Thompson sub-machine guns, three Mills bombs, and a stick of dynamite.[15]

SINGER TO THE UNDERWORLD

Famous Irish playwright, Sean O'Casey, was born and raised in a squalid tenement house in Lower Dorset Street, not too far from

These tenements in Chancery Lane, the Liberties, in early twentieth century were typical of the Liberties and Monto. (Courtesy of Fotofinish)

Monto. The experience of growing up in such conditions had a lasting influence on him. His writings, particularly *The Plough and the Stars*, depict in graphic detail, the place, the people and the times he lived through. He understood the slum world, he respected the residents and workers there, including prostitutes, and expressed their real thoughts in his play. It was said in 1926 by a writer to a newspaper, that O'Casey was a 'singer to the underworld'.

The Plough and the Stars was set around the events prior to and during the 1916 Rising and was first performed in the Abbey Theatre in 1926. *The Plough and the Stars* was a hugely provocative tragicomedy play that challenged the myths, legends and romance that surrounded the 1916 Rising and the War of Independence. One of the important characters in the play is Rosie Redmond, a prostitute, called 'a daughter of the Digs' (Monto) and played by Ria Mooney, a famous Abbey actress. This is an example of O'Casey's provocative style and the Rosie Redmond scene shows

235

Playwright Sean O'Casey with Ria Mooney as the Monto prostitute in the 1926 Abbey Theatre production of *The Plough and the Stars*. O'Casey inscribed the photograph: 'Be clever maid and let who will be good'. (Courtesy of Dublin Forums/MARKD)

her trying to pick up a Monto customer while the voice of Patrick Pearse is heard outside the pub extolling the virtues of nationalism. O'Casey gave her an important role in the play – she was a lightning rod for the tensions that erupted in the course of the play. In one instance she complained to the barman in the Monto pub that a nearby Irish Volunteers meeting was bad for her business. Because of Rosie's role in the play and because the Irish flag was brought into the pub, many in the audience took great umbrage. They felt the 1916 patriots' efforts and memories were being desecrated and defiled. Consequently there was uproar and riots in the theatre during and after the showing. Poet and Nobel Prize winner, William Butler Yeats, famously declared to rioters against the play, 'You have disgraced yourselves again; is this to be the recurring celebration of the arrival of Irish genius?'[16]

EPILOGUE

Today, the Monto area has a defined number of streets and avenues – not many in comparison to the heyday of Monto at the end of the nineteenth century. The dense network of poor dwellings that were very much in evidence in the irregular and many back lanes, courts, and alleyways, secret passages and tenements, were

Child in a Monto tenement in the 1970s, before demolition began. (Courtesy of Dublin Forums/Damntheweather)

demolished by Dublin Corporation in the second half of the twentieth century. Mecklenburgh Lane, Summer Place, Kane's Court, Willet's Cottages, Moore's Cottages, Hamilton's Lane, Breen's Court, Ayre's Court, Carroll's Court, White's Court, Faithful Place, Elliott Place and Brady's Cottages, are no more. Even main streets such as Purdon Street, Mabbot Street, Mecklenburgh and Montgomery Streets, the very heart of Monto, have changed utterly or been demolished.

The notorious reputation of this area, as well as concerted campaigns from strong and committed individuals and local residents and action groups precipitated many changes. New names such as Foley, Railway and James Joyce Street have replaced the old names, and not for the first time, as the City Fathers had changed the names of the principal streets a number of times in the hope of banishing the area of its terrible reputation.

Houses on Summerhill in the early 1960s, before they were demolished. (Courtesy of Dublin Forums/Cosmo)

Corporation Buildings in the 1970s. (Courtesy of GCI/harvest)

As from 2014, we have reason to consider the return or revival of Monto as a possibility. Firstly, prostitution in Ireland is now measured as part of GDP calculations. The Central Statistics Office has set up a dedicated team to measure the earnings of prostitution. It is recognised from UK and Dutch figures that prostitution gives a substantial boost to economies. The government now recognises that Irish figures could help Ireland meet its fiscal targets and boost the economy. Secondly, in recent years Monto has returned to its former activities with the resurgence of prostitution in the area conducted not in old tenements but in private apartments built on the sites of former Georgian houses, and operating behind online shop fronts. Today, two separate campaign groups reflect differing views on whether to ban or legalise prostitution. The Stop the Red Light Campaign and the Stop the Blue Light Campaign are trying to persuade the government to regulate prostitution to greater or lesser degrees. The government's response so far has been to introduce some kind of aspirational legislation and the fight continues. It has been suggested that such is the scale of the earnings from this illicit activity that it will not be long before the government considers putting prostitution on a more legal and regulated footing and that Monto could well be revived. There is even speculation that the former area called Hell might also be reopened for business.

It is still possible to visit the Monto area today to see some of the main streets, surviving pubs and shops, wall plaques, Georgian houses and buildings, alleys and steps, and retrace some of the most pivotal events in modern Irish social, religious, economic and political history, that were played out in this unique area of Dublin, called Monto.

Foley Street (originally called Montgomery Street) in the heart of Monto, 1974. (Courtesy of Dublin Forums/ Damntheweather)

NOTES

CHAPTER 1

1. Gilbert, John, *History of the City of Dublin, Vol.1* (1854), pp.142-145; Lecky, W.E.H., *A History of Ireland in the Eighteenth Century, Vol.1* (1892), p.173; Craig, Maurice, *Dublin 1660–1860: The Shaping of a City* (1952), pp.145-167; Moody, T.W. and Vaughan, W.E., *A New History of Ireland: Eighteenth Century Ireland, Vol.4* (1986), p.105.
2. Maxwell, Constantia, *Dublin under the Georges* (1936), p.78
3. Whitelaw, James, *An Essay on the Population of Dublin, 1798* (1805), p.96.
4. Swift, Jonathan, *A Modest Proposal* (1729), p.23.
5. Gilbert, J.T., *History of the City of Dublin, Vol.1* (1854).p.149.
6. Ball, F.E., *A History of County Dublin* (1905), p.91.
7. Craig, Maurice, *Dublin 1660–1860* (1952), pp.175–190; Lecky, W.E.H., *A History of Ireland in the Eighteenth Century,* Vol.1 (1892), p.207.
8. Curtis, Maurice, *The Liberties: A History* (2013), pp.49-54.
9. Gilbert, J.T., *History of the City of Dublin, Vol.1* (1854); Henry, Brian, *Dublin Hanged: Crime, Law Enforcement and Punishment in late 18th Century Dublin* (1994), p.46; Curtis, Maurice, *The Liberties: A History* (2013); pp.49-54; Bennett, Douglas, *Encyclopaedia of Dublin* (1991).

CHAPTER 2

1. Mac Thomáis, Éamonn, *Me Jewel And Darlin' Dublin* (1998), p.51; *Irish Historic Towns Atlas*; Rocque, John, *Map of Dublin, 1756*.
2. *Irish Historic Towns Atlas no. 19. Dublin Part II, 1610–1756*; *Universal Adventurer*, 11 November 1753; Strangeway, Leonard, R., *The Walls of Dublin from all Available Authorities* (1904), Map of Old Dublin before the work of the Wide Street Commissioners began at end of 18th century.
3. Milne, Ken (ed.), *Christ Church Cathedral Dublin: A History* (2000), p.65.
4. O'Neill, Tim, *Merchants and Mariners in Medieval Ireland* (1987), pp.52–54.
5. Milne, Kenneth (ed.), *Christ Church Cathedral Dublin: A History* (2000), p.87.
6. Gilbert, John, *History of the City of Dublin, Vol.1* (1854), p.145.
7. Section on Dublin churches in the Central Catholic Library.
8. *Guide to Christ Church Cathedral Dublin*, N.D.
9. Rocque, John, *Map of Dublin, 1756*; Moody, T.W. and Vaughan, W.E., *A New History of Ireland: Eighteenth Century Ireland 1691–1800, Vol.4* (1986), p.669; Lennon, Colm and Montague, John, *John Rocque's Dublin: A Guide to a Georgian City* (2010).
10. 'James Annesley' in *Dictionary of National Biography* (1900).
11. Milne Ken (ed.), *Christ Church Cathedral Dublin: A History* (2000) p.128.
12. *Dublin Penny Journal*, Vol.1, No.18, 27 October 1832.
13. Gilbert, John, *History of the City of Dublin, Vol.1* (1854), p.140.

CHAPTER 3

1. Office of Public Works, *St Audoen's Church*, N.D.
2. ibid.
3. Costello, Peter, *Churches of Dublin* (1989) is a very useful guide and commentary of major churches; Section on Parishes in Central Catholic Library.
4. Dublin City Council, *Walls of Dublin*, N.D.
5. Gilbert, John, *History of the City of Dublin, Vol.1* (1854), p.98.

6. Lennon, Colm and Montague, John, *John Rocque's Dublin: A Guide to a Georgian City* (2010), Introduction.

CHAPTER 4

1 *Irish Historic Towns Atlas*; Rocque, John, *Map of Dublin, 1756*.

2. Joyce, Weston St John, *The Neighbourhood of Dublin* (1912), p.60.

3. Gilbert, John, *History of the City of Dublin, Vol.1* (1854), p.176.

4. Morash, Christopher, *Smock Alley Theatre*, N.D; *Irish Historic Towns Atlas*; Rocque, John, *Map of Dublin, 1756*.

5. Gilbert, *John, History of the City of Dublin, Vol.1* (1854), p.87; Comerford, Revd Patrick, blog http://comerfordfamily.blogspot.ie/2007/12/welcome-to-comerford-family-history.html

6. Comerford, Revd Patrick, blog http://comerfordfamily.blogspot.ie/2007/12/welcome-to-comerford-family-history.html; Gilbert, John, *History of the City of Dublin, Vol.1* (1854), p.139.

7. Joyce, Weston St John, *The Neighbourhood of Dublin* (1912), p.34.

8. *Irish Historic Towns Atlas*; Rocque, John, *Map of Dublin, 1756*.

CHAPTER 5

1. *Irish Historic Towns Atlas*; Rocque, John, *Map of Dublin, 1756*; McCready, Revd C.T., *Dublin Street Names* (1887), p.34.

2. Fitzpatrick, William J., *The Sham Squire and the Informers of 1798* (1869), p.62.

CHAPTER 6

1. Luddy, Maria, *Prostitution and Irish Society, 1800–1940* (2007), pp.33-35; Kelly, James, *Sport in Ireland 1600–1840* (2014), p.112; Harris, A.N., *Harris's Guide to Convent Garden Ladies* (1788), p.98; Rutherford, David, 'An Age of Innocence: Prostitution in Victorian London' in Hackwriters.com, N.D.

2. Lyons, Mary (Ed.), *The Memoirs of Mrs Leeson, Madam 1727–1797* (1995), pp.vi–xix; Luddy, Marie, *Prostitution and Irish Society 1800–1940* (2007), pp.33–35.

3. Henry, Brian, *Dublin Hanged: Crime, Law Enforcement and Punishment in Late 18th Century Ireland* (1994), pp.37–60.

4. Harding's Hotel, Fishamble Street, Dublin; Hopkins, Frank, *Hidden Dublin: Deadbeats, Dossers and Decent Skins* (2008), p.37.

5. For additional information on the legend of Darkey Kelly, thanks to McLoughlin, Eamon and O'Grady, Philip of 3fm; O'Keefe, Alan of *The Herald*, Irish Central and the staff at the Hardings Hotel.

6. Curtis, Maurice, *The Liberties: A History* (2013), p.142.

7. Leeson, Margaret, *Memoirs of Mrs Margaret Leeson*, 3 Vols (1797); Lyons, Mary (ed.), *The Memoirs of Mrs Leeson, Madam 1727–1797* (1995), pp.vi–xix; Moynihan, Karyn, 'Peg Plunkett', article from the *Woman's Museum of Ireland* (2012); O'Reilly, Niamh, 'Prostitutes' and 'Three Hundred Years of Vice', article from *Estudios Irlandeses* by Niamh O'Reilly of the Global Women's Studies Programme at NUI Galway (2008).

8. Moynihan, Karyn, 'Peg Plunkett', article from the *Woman's Museum of Ireland* (2012); O'Reilly, Niamh, 'Prostitutes' and 'Three Hundred Years of Vice', article from *Estudios Irlandeses* by Niamh O'Reilly of the Global Women's Studies Programme at NUI Galway (2008).

9. O'Reilly, Niamh, 'Prostitutes' and 'Three Hundred Years of Vice', article from *Estudios Irlandeses* by Niamh O'Reilly of the Global Women's Studies Programme at NUI Galway (2008).

10. Lyons, Mary (ed.), *Memoirs of Margaret Leeson, Madam 1727–1797* (1995), Introduction.

11. Leeson, Margaret, *Memoirs of Mrs Margaret Leeson*, 3 Vols (1797).

12. Lyons, Mary (ed.), *Memoirs of Margaret Leeson, Madam 1727–1797* (1995), p.79; Leeson, Margaret, *Memoirs of Mrs Margaret Leeson*, 3 Vols (1797); Luddy, Marie, *Prostitution and Irish Society, 1800–1940* (2007), pp.33-35.

CHAPTER 7

1 Ball, Francis Erlington, *A History of the County Dublin* (1905), p.39; Fewer, Michael, *The Wicklow Military road; History and Topography* (2008); Curtis, Maurice, *Rathfarnham* (2013), p.83.

2. Fewer, Michael, 'The Hellfire Club, Co. Dublin' in *History Ireland*, Vol.18, No.3 (May–June 2010), p.29.

3. Gilbert, John, *History of the City of Dublin Vol.1* (1854), p.16–17; Dún Laoghaire-Rathdown County Council, *Did You Know…? Forgotten Aspects of our Local Heritage* (2009).

4. Fewer, Michael, 'The Hellfire Club, Co. Dublin' in *History Ireland*, Vol.18, No.3 (May–June 2010), p.29.

5. Fewer, Michael, 'The Hellfire Club, Co. Dublin' in *History Ireland*, Vol.18, No.3 (May–June 2010), p.29; Ryan, David, *Blasphemers and Blackguards: The Irish Hellfire Clubs* (2012), p.98; Hammond, J.W., *The Story of Killakee House and the Hellfire Club*, N.D.; Hammond, J.W., *The Hellfire Club*, N.D.; Lord, Evelyn, *The Hellfire Club: Sex, Satanism and Secret Societies* (2008), p.90.

6. Fewer, Michael, 'The Hellfire Club, Co. Dublin' in *History Ireland*, Vol.18, No.3 (May–June 2010), p.29.

7. Handcock, William Domville, *The History and Antiquities of Tallaght in the County of Dublin* (1876). p.43; Healy, Patrick, 'Glenasmole Roads' (pdf) (South Dublin Libraries, (2006).

8. Tracy, Frank, 'If Those Trees Could Speak: The Story of an Ascendancy Family in Ireland' (pdf); *Dublin: South Dublin Libraries* (2005), p.6.

9. Fewer, Michael, 'The Hellfire Club, Co. Dublin' in *History Ireland*, Vol.18, No.3 (May–June 2010), p.29.

CHAPTER 8

1. *Dublin Penny Journal*, 1832.

2 *Dublin Penny Journal*, 1832; Gilbert, John, *History of the City of Dublin, Vol.1* (1854), p.93.

CHAPTER 9

1. Dublin City Archives, Catalogue from Battersby's Auctioneers belonging to the Collection of Sir Compton Meade Domvile, 1944– In Hellfire Club File.

2. Fr John Gwynn biography in Irish Room of CCL; Ordnance Survey Ireland, No. 50: Dublin, Kildare, Meath, Wicklow (Map) 1:50,000, Discovery Series (6th edition) (2010).

3 There are a number of guides to Christ Church Cathedral in the Central Catholic Library.

4. Lord, Evelyn, and Ryan, David, have written extensively of the Irish and English Hellfire Clubs.

CHAPTER 10

1. Luddy, Maria, *Prostitution and Irish Society, 1800–1940* (2007), p.33-35.
2. ibid., p.17.
3. ibid.
4. *United Service Journal*, 1837. Donal Fallon/Comeheretome.
5. Curtis, Maurice, *Portobello* (2011), p.49.
6. Costello, Con, *The Curragh Wrens*, N.D., p.2.
7. Ferriter, Diarmuid in *Irish Examiner*, 1 November 2007; Costello, Con, *The Curragh Wrens*, N.D.; Greenwood, James, *The Seven Curses of London* (1869), p.41; Malone, Martin, *Rosanna Nightwalker: The Wren of the Curragh*, N.D., p.3; James Greenwood articles in the *Pall Mall Gazette*, 1867; Luddy, M., *Prostitution and Irish Society, 1800–1940* (2007), pp.33-35.
8. Luddy, M., *Prostitution and Irish Society, 1800–1940* (2007), pp.33-35.

CHAPTER 11

1. *Freeman's Journal*, 29 March 1865.
2. Finegan, John, *The Story of Monto* (1978), p.21; MacThomáis, Éamonn, *Me Jewel and Darlin' Dublin* (1998), p.45.
3. Armstrong, Maggie, 'The Bloomsday world tourists never get to hear about', *Irish Independent*, 21 June 201; Pierse, Michael, 'A tale of two cities', *An Phoblacht, Irish Republican News*, 20 November 2000; Pierse, Michael, 'The Miracle of Monto', *An Phoblacht, Irish Republican News*, 5 September 2002.
4. Fagan, Terry (and the North Inner City Folklore Project), *Monto: Madams, Murder and Black Coddle* (2000); Finegan, John, *The Story of Monto* (1978), pp.15-20; Luddy, Maria, *Prostitution and Irish Society, 1800–1940* (2007), pp.33-35.

CHAPTER 12

1. Bennet, Douglas, *The Encyclopaedia of Dublin* (1991); McCready, Revd C.T., *Dublin Street Names Dated and Explained* (1898); Ball, Francis E., *A History of the County Dublin* (1906), p.91.

2. McCready, C.T., *Dublin Street Names Dated and Explained* (1898), p.46; Ball, Francis E., *A History of the County Dublin* (1906), p75.

3. Gardiner, Luke, *A Cambridge Alumni Database*, retrieved 26 June 2014; McCready, Revd C.T., *Dublin Street Names Dated and Explained* (1898), p.38; Ball, Francis E., *A History of the County Dublin* (1906), p.81.

4. Gardiner, Luke, A Cambridge Alumni Database, retrieved 26 June 2014; The Irish Georgian Society, City Assembly House, 58 South William Street, Dublin 2; McCready, C.T., *Dublin Street Names Dated and Explained* (1898), p.72; Ball, Francis E., *A History of the County Dublin* (1906), p.83.

5. McCready, C.T., *Dublin Street Names Dated and Explained* (1898), p.101; Ball, Francis E., *A History of the County Dublin* (1906), p.70.

6. Boylan, Henry, *A Dictionary of Irish Biography* (1978); McCready, C.T., *Dublin Street Names Explained* (1898), p.34.

7. Craig, Maurice, *Dublin 1660–1860: The Shaping of a City* (1952), p.102.

8. Lyons, Mary (ed.), *The Memoirs of Mrs Leeson, Madam 1727–1797* (199), p.72.

9. Dublin City Libraries/Archives, Gloucester Street Information; Savage, Ben and Fagan, Terry, *All Around the Diamond* (1991), p.14.

10. Fagan, Terry and the North Inner City Folklore Project have done much research and published a number of books and booklets on this area in the past 30 years; McCready, C.T., *Dublin Street Names Dated and Explained* (1898), p.21; Ball, Francis E., *A History of the County Dublin* (1906), p.37.

CHAPTER 13

1. Finegan, John, *The Story of Monto* (1978), p.10; Fagan, Terry and the North Inner City Folklore Project, *Monto: Madams, Murder and Black Coddle* (2000), p.16.

2. Census for Dublin, 1911.

3. Gogarty, Oliver St John, *As I Was Going Down Sackville Street* (1937), p.102; Gogarty, Oliver St John, *Tumbling in the Hay* (1939), p.90; O'Connor, Ulick, *Oliver St John Gogarty* (1963); Fagan, Terry and the North Inner City Folklore Project, *Monto: Madams, Murder and Black Coddle* (2000), p.28; Finegan, John, *The Story of Monto* (1978), pp. 6-10.

4. Fagan, Terry and the North Inner City Folklore Project, *Dublin Tenements* (2013), p.8; Curtis, Maurice, *The Challenge to Democracy: Militant Catholicism in Modern Ireland* (2010), pp.66-7, 72,75; Jacinta Prunty, *Dublin Slums 1800–1925* (1998), p.112..

5. Fagan, Terry and the North Inner City Folklore Project, *Dublin Tenements* (2013), p.2.

6. Finegan, John, *The Story of Monto* (1978), p.12; Fagan, Terry and the North Inner City Folklore Project, *Monto: Madams, Murder and Black Coddle* (2000), p.5.

CHAPTER 14

1. Finegan, John, *The Story of Monto* (1978), p.18; Fagan, Terry and the North Inner City Folklore Project, *Monto: Madams, Murder and Black Coddle* (2000), p.11; Ellman, Richard, *James Joyce* (1959), p.312; *Thom's Directories 1880–1925*; Beck, Harold & Simpson, Mark, James Joyce online notes (2013).

2. Gogarty, Oliver St John, *As I Was Going Down Sackville Street* (1937), p. 266; Gogarty, Oliver St John, *Tumbling in the Hay* (1939), p.112.

3. Finegan, John, *The Story of Monto* (1978), p.11; Fagan, Terry and the North Inner City Folklore Project, *Monto: Madams, Murder and Black Coddle* (2000), p.32; *Thom's Directories*.

4. Beck, Harold and Simpson, Mark, James Joyce online notes (2013).

5. Beck, Harold and Simpson, Mark, James Joyce online notes, (2013); Duff, Frank, *Miracles on Tap* (1961), p.73; Frank Duff Interview (1979); *Thom's Directories*.

6. Census of Ireland, 1901; *Thom's Directory* (1887); Beck, Harold and Simpson, Mark, James Joyce online notes, 2013.

7. Gogarty, Oliver St John, *Tumbling in the Hay* (1939), Chapter 22, pp.251–268; *Thom's Directory*, 1887.

8. *Freeman's Journal*, 23 May 1865.

9. Beck, Harold and Simpson, Mark, James Joyce online notes (2013).

10. ibid.

11. Gogarty, Oliver St John, *As I Was Going Down Sackville Street* (1937), p. 301.
12. O'Connor, Ulick, *Oliver St. John Gogarty: A Poet and his Times* (1964), p.55.
13. O'Connor, Ulick picks this up in his *Oliver St. John Gogarty: A Poet and his Times* (1964), p. 55.
14. *Freeman's Journal*, August 1887.
15. Beck, Harold & Simpson, Mark, James Joyce online notes (2013); Joyce, James, *Ulysses* (1922).

CHAPTER 15

1. Finegan, John, *The Story of Monto* (1978), p.23; Fagan, Terry and the North Inner City Folklore Project, *Monto: Madams, Murder and Black Coddle* (2000), p.19.
2. Luddy, Maria, *Prostitution and Irish Society 1800–1940* (2007), pp.33-35.
3. Finegan, John, *The Story of Monto* (1978), p.11; Fagan, Terry and the North Inner City Folklore Project, *Monto: Madams, Murder and Black Coddle* (2000), p.19; Duff, Frank, *Miracles on Tap* (1961), p.89.
4. Terry Fagan, *Dublin Tenements* (2013), p.86.
5. Gogarty, Oliver St John, *As I Was Going Down Sackville Street* (1937), pp. 264–266.
6. Fagan, Terry and the North Inner City Folklore Project, *Monto: Madams, Murder and Black Coddle* (2000), p.17; Terry Fagan, *Dublin Tenements* (2013), p.23; Duff, Frank, *Miracles on Tap* (1961), p.54.
7. Luddy, Maria, *Prostitution and Irish Society 1800–1940* (2007), pp. 125–155; The Skibbereen Eagle: Dublin, Lepers, Lock and Clap, 30 October 2012.
8. Duff, Frank, *Miracles on Tap* (1961), p.90; Frank Duff Interview, 1979.
9. Duff, Frank, *Miracles on Tap* (1961), p.92; Frank Duff Interview, 1979.
10. Hughes, Patricia, *Who Killed Honor Bright?* (c. 2009).
11. Prunty, Jacinta, *Dublin Slums 1800–1925* (1998), pp. 263–270.
12. McCarthy, Michael, *Priests and People in Ireland* (1902), p 82.

CHAPTER 16

1. *Freeman's Journal*, August 1911.
2. Luddy, Maria, *Prostitution and Irish Society 1800–1940* (2007), pp.125–155, 157–158, 169, 173.
3. ibid., p. 40.
4. Curtis, Maurice, *Challenge to Democracy: Militant Catholicism in Modern Ireland* (2010), pp.65-68.
5. Duff, Frank, *Miracles on Ta*p (1961), p. 121; Frank Duff Interview, 1979; Curtis, Maurice, *Challenge to Democracy: Militant Catholicism in Modern Ireland* (2010), p.65-68.
6. Curtis, Maurice, *Challenge to Democracy: Militant Catholicism in Modern Ireland* (2010), p.65-68.
7. Duff, Frank, *Miracles on Tap* (1961), p.91.
8. *Irish Independent*, 13 March, 1925; *Cork Examiner*, 13 March, 1925.
9. Curtis, Maurice, *Challenge to Democracy. Militant Catholicism in Modern Ireland* (2010), p.65-68.
10. Duff, Frank, *Miracles on Tap* (1961), p.98; Finegan, John, *The Story of Monto* (1978), p.29; Fagan, Terry and the North Inner City Folklore Project, *Monto: Madams, Murder and Black Coddle* (2000), p.34.

CHAPTER 17

1. Report of the Dublin Disturbances Commission, 1914.
2. *The Irish Times*, 11 April 2014; Joe Duffy's List of Children Killed in 1916 Rising: http://static.rasset.ie/documents/radio1/joe-duffys-list-of-children-killed-in-1916-rising.pdf.
3. Finegan, John, *The Story of Monto* (1978), pp.16-17; Fagan, Terry and the North Inner City Folklore Project, *Monto: Madams, Murder and Black Coddle* (2000), p.28; Breen, Dan, *My Fight for Irish Freedom* (1993), p.59; Gogarty, Oliver St John, *As I Was Going Down Sackville Street* (1937), p.266; Gogarty, Oliver St John, *Tumbling in the Hay* (1939); Connell, Joseph E.A., *Dublin in Rebellion: A Directory 1913–1923* (2006), p.12.
4. Breen, Dan, *My Fight for Irish Freedom* (1993), p.60; *The Irish Times*, 7 February 1921.
5. White, O'Shea and Younghusband, *Irish Volunteer Soldiers Notes*

1913–1923 (2003), p.101; Connell, Joseph E.A., *Dublin in Rebellion: A Directory 1913–1923* (2006), p.46.

CHAPTER 18

1. Joyce, John Stanislaus, *My Brother's Keeper* (1958), p.154.
2. Finegan, John, *The Story of Monto* (1978), p.20.
3. Luddy, Maria, *Prostitution and Irish Society 1800–1940* (2007), pp.33-35; Joyce, James, *Ulysses* (1922), p.470 and 'Circe' chapter at pp.425–533. Joyce, James, *Portrait of the Artist as a Young Man* (1916), pp.102–196.
4. Ellmann, Richard, *James Joyce* (1959), pp.367–368; Gilbert, Stuart, James Joyce, *Ulysses* (1955), pp.313–348.
5. 'Joyce syphilis claim splits scholars', *The Sunday Times*, 8 June 2014; Fr Bruce Bradley S.J., Ian Pinder and David Norris talking about James Joyce; James Joyce, *Ulysses* (1955), pp.313–348.
6. David Norris and Ian Pinder talking about James Joyce; Ellmann, Richard, *James Joyce* (1959), pp.367–368.
7. Joyce, James, *Portrait of the Artist as a Young Man* (1916), p.223.
8. ibid., pp.105–106; Joyce, James, *Ulysses* (1922), p.438; Ellmann, Richard, *James Joyce* (1959), pp.367–68; James Joyce, *Ulysses* (1955), pp.313–48.
9. David Norris talking about James Joyce; Ellmann, Richard, *James Joyce* (1959), pp. 67–368.
10. Joyce, James, *Ulysses* (1922), p. 470 and 'Circe' chapter at pp.425–533; Ellmann, Richard, *James Joyce* (1959), pp.367–368.
11. Gogarty, Oliver St John, *Tumbling in the Hay* (1939), p.260.
12. ibid.
13. Gogarty, Oliver St John, *As I Was Going Down Sackville Street* (1937), p. 285.
14. O'Flaherty, Liam, *The Informer* (1925), p.61.
15. Behan, Brendan, *The Quare Fellow* (1954), p 78.
16. Sean O'Casey, *The Plough and the Stars* (1926), p. 20.

FURTHER READING

Ashe, Geoffrey, *The Hell-Fire Clubs. Sex, Rakes and Libertines* (second edition) (London; Sutton Publishing Ltd, 2005)

Ball, Francis Erlington, *A History of the County Dublin* Part 3 (Dublin; Alex Thom & Co., 1905) Pdf, retrieved 9 August 2010

Barry, Michael and Sammon, Patrick *Dublin's Strangest Tales* (2013)

Beck, Harold and Simpson, Mark, *James Joyce Online Notes* (2013)

Bennett, Douglas, *Encyclopaedia of Dublin* (1991)

Clarke, Desmond, *Dublin* (1977)

Clarke, Howard (ed.), *Medieval Dublin: The Making of a Metropolis* (2012)

Connell, Joseph E.A., *Dublin in Rebellion: A Directory 1913–1923* (2006)

Cosgrove, Ar, *Dublin Through the Ages* (1986)

Costello, Peter, *James Joyce: The Years of Growth, 1882–1915* (1994)

Costello, Peter, *Dublin Churches* (1989)

Craig, Maurice, *Dublin 1660–1860: The Shaping of a City* (1952)

Curtis, Maurice, *The Challenge to Democracy: Militant Catholicism in Modern Ireland* (2008)

Curtis, Maurice, *Rathmines* (2010)

Curtis, Maurice, *Portobello* (2011)

Curtis, Maurice, *The Liberties* (2013)

Curtis, Maurice, *Rathfarnham* (2013)

Curtis, Maurice, *Glasnevin* (2014)

Daly, Mary, Pearson, Peter and Hearn, Mona, *Dublin's Victorian Houses* (1998)

Daly, Mary E., *Dublin - The Deposed Capital* (1984)

Dún Laoghaire-Rathdown County Council, *Did You Know ... ? Forgotten Aspects of our Local Heritage* (Dublin: Dún Laoghaire-Rathdown County Council, 2009)

Ellmann, Richard, *James Joyce* (1959)

Fagan, Terry (and the North Inner City Folklore Project), *Monto: Madams, Murder and Black Coddle* (2000)

Fagan, Terry and McKeever, Gerry (ed.)/North Inner City Folklore, *Dublin Tenements* (2013)

Fagan, Terry and Savage, Ben (eds), *All around the Diamond* (1994)

Fagan, Terry and Savage, Ben (eds), *Those were the Days* (1992)

Fewer, Michael, *The Wicklow Military Road. History and Topography* (2007)

Fewer, Michael, 'The Hellfire Club, Co. Dublin' in *History Ireland* Vol.18, No.3 (May–June 2010), p. 29

Finegan, John, *The Story of Monto* (1978)

Fourwinds, Tom, *Monumental About: Prehistoric Dublin* (Dublin; 2006)

Gilbert, John, *History of the City of Dublin*, 3 Vols (1854)

Gilbert. John, *The Streets of Dublin* (1852)

Gilbert, Stuart, *James Joyce's Ulysses* (1955)

Gogarty, Oliver St John, *Tumbling in the Hay* (1937)

Gogarty, Oliver St John, *As I Walked Down Sackville Street* (1939)

Handcock, William Domville, *The History and Antiquities of Tallaght in the County of Dublin* (second edition, 1991) (first published 1876)

Healy, Patrick, *Glenasmole Roads* (pdf) (Dublin: South Dublin Libraries, 2006)

Hopkins, Frank, *Hidden Dublin: Deadbeats, Dossers and Decent Skins* (2008)

Joyce, James, *Portrait of the Artist as a Young Man* (1916)

Joyce, James, *Ulysses* (1922)

Joyce, Weston St John, *The Neighbourhood of Dublin* (1939) (First published 1912)

Kearns, Kevin C., *Dublin Tenements: An Oral History* (1994)

Kearns, Kevin C., *Dublin Voices: An Oral Folk History* (1998)

Kelly, James, *The Liberty and Ormond Boys: Factional Riot in eighteenth-century Dublin* (2005)

Kelly, Alderman Thomas Kelly, T.D., *The Streets of Dublin 1910–1911* (2013)

Killeen, Richard, *Historical Atlas of Dublin* (2009)

Killeen, Richard, *A Short History of Dublin* (2010)

Lecky, W.E.H., *A History of Ireland in the Eighteenth Century* Vol.1 (1892)

Large, Peter Somerville, *Dublin* (1979)

Lennon, Colm and Montague, John, *John Rocque's Dublin: A Guide to a Georgian City* (2010)

Liddy, Pat, *Dublin: A Celebration, From the 1st to the 21st Century* (2000)

Lord, Evelyn, *The Hell-Fire Clubs: Sex, Satanism and Secret Societies* (2008)

Luddy, M., *Prostitution and Irish Society, 1800–1940* (2007)

Lyons, Mary (ed.), *The Memoirs of Mrs Leeson, Madam 1727–1797* (1995)

MacDonald, Frank, *The Destruction of Dublin* (1985)

MacThomáis, Éamonn, *Gur Cake and Coal Blocks* (1976)

MacThomáis, Éamonn, *Janey Mac Me Shirt is Black* (1974)

MacThomáis, Éamonn, *Me Jewel and Darling Dublin* (1974)

Maxwell, Constantia, *Dublin Under the Georges 1714–1830* (1936)

Milne, Kenneth (ed.), *Christ Church Cathedral Dublin: A History* (2010)

O'Connor, Ulick, *Oliver St John Gogarty* (1963)

O'Farrell, Padraic, *Irish GhoStories* (2004)

O'Flaherty, Liam, *The Informer* (1925)

Ordnance Survey Ireland, *No. 50: Dublin, Kildare, Meath, Wicklow* (Map), 1:50,000. Discovery Series (sixth edition) (2010)

Pearson, Peter, *The Heart of Dublin* (2000)

Prunty, Jacinta, *Dublin Slums, 1800–925* (1998)

Ryan, David, *Blasphemers & Blackguards: The Irish Hellfire Clubs* (2012)

Savage, Ben and Fagan, Terry, *All Around the Diamond* (1991)

Savage, Ben and Fagan, Terry, *Memories from Corporation Buildings and Foley Street*, N.D.

Somerville-Large, Peter, *Dublin* (1979)

Tracy, Frank, *If Those Trees Could Speak. The Story of an Ascendancy Family in Ireland* (pdf) (2005)

Walsh, Dave, *Haunted Dublin* (2008)

Whitelaw, Revd James, *An Essay on the Population of Dublin, 1798* (1805)

If you enjoyed this book, you may also be interested in...

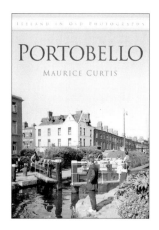

Portobello In Old Photographs
MAURICE CURTIS

In this book, Maurice Curtis, takes the reader on a visual tour of Portobello through the decades, recounting both the familiar and the events and places that have faded over time, revealing many fascinating details, including the fact that Dublin's Portobello was named after an area on the East Coast of Panama! This, and much more, is captured in a timeless volume, which pays fitting tribute to this well-loved part of the city.

978 1 84588 737 7

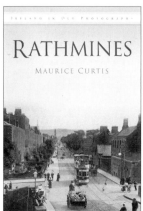

Rathmines In Old Photographs
MAURICE CURTIS

Rathmines is one of the country's most well-known suburbs, home to heads of government, vast swathes of students and local families alike. In his latest book, writer and historian Maurice Curtis takes the reader on a visual tour of Rathmines through the decades, recounting both the familiar and the forgotten, those features and events that may have faded over time. Illustrated with over 150 archive photographs, this fascinating book pays fitting tribute to the place Rathmines has carved in the history of all who have passed through it.

978 1 84588 704 9

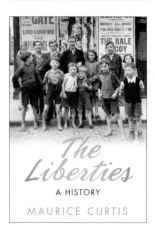

The Liberties
MAURICE CURTIS

Following the murder of Thomas á Becket, King Henry II decreed that an abbey be founded close to the present-day St Catherine's church, Thomas Street, Dublin, in Becket's memory, and the monks that founded it were to be free from city taxes and rates. This 'Liberty' expanded and took in the part of Dublin which today is known as the Liberties, one of Dublin's oldest and most interesting parts of the capital. In this book, author Maurice Curtis explores this fascinating history and its significance to the people of Dublin.

978 1 84588 771 1

Visit our websites and discover hundreds of other History Press books.

www.thehistorypress.ie www.thehistorypress.co.uk